PRINCIPLES
FOR
ETHICS
IN
BUSINESS

REVISED EDITION

W. L. LaCroix, S. J.

University Press
of America™

Copyright © 1979 by

University Press of America, Inc.™

4710 Auth Place, S.E., Washington D.C. 20023

ISBN: 0-8191-0452-3

Library of Congress Catalog Card Number: 78-59855

ACKNOWLEDGEMENTS:

Work on this book was assisted by help from

the Rossner Fund, the Lilly Foundation, and

a Rockhurst Presidential Grant.

CONTENTS

INTRODUCTION: SPECIFIC PRINCIPLES FOR BUSINESS

Peter Drucker writes: "But there is neither a separate ethics of business, nor is one needed."[1] He goes on, however, to argue that, because they are members in the leadership groups of the society of organizations, business managers can face peculiar ethical problems that differ from their problems as private individuals.[2] If this is true, then as these managers handle these ethical problems peculiar to business, they will use some principles other than those they use as private individuals. Therefore, here is an area for separate investigation: the specific principles for ethics peculiar to business.

It certainly is fashionable to speak of "business ethics." Events of the 1970's have altered the consciousness of people in their evaluation of business leaders. In 1966, a Lou Harris poll reported that 55 percent of the people had strong confidence in the heads of large corporations. By 1974, this had dropped to 21 percent, and by 1976 to 16 percent. The Daniel Yankelovich survey reported that the proportion of the public that thought business struck a fair balance between profits and the public interest dropped from 70 percent in 1968 to 20 percent in 1974. A Gallup poll in 1975 reported that, among institutions comprising "the U.S. power structure," big business came in last with a confidence score of 34 percent and stood behind organized labor, Congress, the Supreme Court, the Executive branch, the military, education, and organized religion.

A factor in the inability of business leaders to impress people with their actions today is that, in matters of business practice, few seem to be certain of the ethical right and wrong. The first step toward clarification here is to distinguish "malpractice in business" into three areas: "white collar crime," unethical kinds of individual actions, and unethical kinds of business actions.

Business ethics does not directly treat of the first two. It does not treat (1) the illegal "white collar crimes" by individuals or organizations, such as those activities of bribery, expressed price-fixing, lying to misrepresent a contract exchange, falsification of data, which are addressed by positive laws already established in society; or (2) the acts of individuals who, while in business positions, do things that are unethical in ways not specific to business, such as running down the reputation of another to gain promotional advantage, embezzlement, or varieties of "ripping off."

1

Business ethics does not directly treat these two areas because the ethical principles for their evaluation arise primarily in contexts not specific to business. Principles for them arise in reflection on the function of positive law in society and in reflection on private, interpersonal ethics. Business ethics must treat the Business System itself. It must clarify principles involved in the system as it actually works, as it involves and affects human decisions and values.

If the only valid ethical principles were those of personal ethics, then in practice people would have no choice but to separate personal ethics and the activities and goals of business, with the result that personal ethics often would be "compromised" in favor of the requirements that are reasonably unavoidable in business.[3] Moreover, the only other source for judgment on business decisions, besides business requirements, would be those requirements of penal law. But the attitude toward penal law would be of the "watch out for the traffic cop" kind, the attitude of the legal positivist who so separates morals and legal prescriptions that one is encouraged to circumvent the laws limited only by the prudential command: "Don't get caught." It could even be acceptable occasionally to get caught as long as the company on the whole is better off. (This is the attitude taught by many professional sports today, and taken to its logical extreme, was symbolized in the gangster movies of the 1930's. See Chapter Three.)

It is the position in this book that there are principles for an ethics specific to business. The position presupposes that one can speak of the institution of business as a system and also as a subsystem in society as a whole. This dual existence means that business has rules for its operations as a business and also has rules for its relations to other operations in society, and both of these have ethical principles. One may state the following as the "charter" for business ethics:

"Whatever business actions, policies and practices have significant impact on the business institution itself or on the lives of people in the society are proper subject matter for business ethics."

To have substance and specification, business ethics must study the practices that function in the business institution, and what values are thereby supported or harmed; and business ethics must study the relationships that pertain for the business institution as a subsystem of the whole social system that is the living society, and what values are thereby supported or harmed.

Thus business ethics has a bileveled aim: to study the ethics of business itself and to study the ethics of business as a

part in the social whole. We might designate these two levels
for questions and evaluations as "the ethics of business under
the horizon of business" ((business as a system, or business in
itself)); and "the ethics of business under the horizon of society" ((business as a subsystem, or business as part of the
social whole)).

To say "That's just good business," or "That's the name of
the game in business," or "If you can't stand the heat, get out
of the kitchen"---is to make a statement in the horizon of business as a system.

To say "The business of America is business," or "Free enterprise is good for the country," or "The business of business
is business"---is to make a statement in the horizon of business
as a subsystem.

Of course, for very few problems can we classify neatly
under which horizon fall the more important questions or evaluations. Usually any problem will lead us back and forth from
a position under one horizon to a position under the other.
However, it is important to make the distinction, because the
dynamics of society gradually may influence a heretofore ethically acceptable practice in business under the business horizon and in time change it to an unethical practice.

Such a bileveled aim today for business ethics developed
as the positive side of the erosion of two earlier attitudes
about the ethical ramifications of decisions and practices in
business. In the past, people presumed that common sense judgment, "intuition," with its rather vaguely understood values of
justice and equality and its rather simplistic patterns by which
to classify situations, was clear enough and applicable for all
the serious and the repetitive ethical problems encountered in
business.

Also in the past, people presumed the reciprocity between
the economic model for good business decisions and the ethical
dimensions of business decisions. Thus they could separate by
a sanitary cordon the principles of all such decisions from the
principles of any decider's ethical non-business life.

At present, the lack of conformity between the set of ethical difficulties of business as a system and the set of ethical
difficulties of business as a subsystem gives rise to what many
call "gray areas" in business ethics. The degrees and lines of
ethical responsibility and the measure and classification of the
effects of actions and procedures need much more cooperative
effort before the light of principled thought can validate the
judgments that now take place in these gray areas. The ethician

4

knows that in the dusk of dawn one prudently steps slowly. If
people in business itself who are serious about ethical behavior hesitate to settle on standards which are specific to business, perhaps all an individual ethician can hope to do is to
contribute to this cooperative effort.

Yet the ethician must insist upon a few touchstones. One
must work out clearly for oneself which human values one most
especially watches in reference to the consequences of business
activities. One must think through the horizons that obtain and
the principles that operate in ethical decisions for business.
However, all this demands only that each person take seriously
all the ethical implications and dimensions of one's actions.
That this is the case is the presupposition of any study of
business ethics.

A NOTE ON THE PERSPECTIVE OF A PHILOSOPHER

If one is working well, a philosopher has "no title." If
one is working well, a philosopher shows tendencies neither to
the right nor to the left, neither liberal nor conservative.
"To have no title" means that one has no presuppositions to remain hidden and no final position to defend.

A philosopher seeks to learn and to articulate by questioning the thoughts of others and oneself. At times, others
may interpret a part of this questioning as an indication that
the philosopher does indeed "have a title." Deep down, a philosopher always hopes that these others have made a mistake. But
if one has in fact betrayed the work at hand, deep down the
philosopher would be glad to be reproved.

CHAPTER ONE

THE ETHICAL HERITAGE IN AMERICAN BUSINESS

As we reflect on business activities in our society, we
acknowledge right at the start the historically unprecedented
economic benefits that members of our society enjoy from our
economic system. On the average, we live today with the highest
standards of material benefits we ever have had, and one of the
highest in history. Those who wish to evaluate strictly on the
"utility" of a system, on its consequences in a certain dimension, would give our business system very high economic marks.
And the evidence is that all the increases in standard of living
for Americans in the last thirty years is the result less of
political planning than of economic growth.

However, also from a "utility" perspective, there are other
consequences that might support negative judgments on the system:
questionable distribution of benefits; waste and deliberate underengineering; the absence of the "full human point of view" in
the attitudes produced; the kinds of motives inculcated and the
limited interpretation of what is meant by "success"; and the
values omitted with emphasis on technological efficiency.

How then do we evaluate what we do in business? How far
do the negative judgments indicate substantial objections? Remember, a system may have many good phases and much good in its
consequences without being ethically satisfactory.

In this chapter, we will review some elements in the ethical evaluations on business made in American history. The premise for such an historical review simply is this: the present
system and its evaluations are the outgrowths of the past, with
both ways to interpret what business goals and means should be,
and historical alternations of these ways to interpret. Two of
the clues uncovered are most important. First, the ethical interpretations on business in the past had certain presuppositions
in models for society and in ideas about justice. Because of
these presuppositions, the actual ethical judgments often seemed
self-evident, but were not. Second, never until our time has
there been a consensus that ethics in business were simply a
combination of personal morality and penal law.

In the last 200 years, American business leaders and American society often shared a body of social and economic philosophy which provided both goals and ethical justification for
many business activities. Writers such as Max Weber, R. H. Tawney and Kenneth Boulding have written of the mutual influence of

5

religious world views, character ideals, and economic values.

In the High Middle Ages, people shared a world view of a
static and hierarchical society in which each person had a
place and justice was in terms of distribution of all social
goods proportionately to place. Incentive rewards for economic
behavior were underplayed in favor of justice meted out by interpreting the phrase "to each one's own" according to one's
place in the social organism. In theory and in social thought
there was hostility toward free and incentively rewarded business. In theory this hostility was based on a dualistic concept of the meaning of human life. There was a "this world-
other world" tension, with the identification of the source of
all human misery in the mistaken inversion that made "this
world" more significant. Business was suspect because it fos-
tered the pursuit of material gain in a manner that divided
persons against each other in the commercial transactions.

With Renaissance and Reformation thought, people gradually
abandoned restrictions on commercial development, not only in
fact but also in theory. The hierarchical society was displaced
by a dynamic and innovative model wherein individuals all did
their parts to develop the economic milieu. Two aspects in this
change are important for us. (1) The idea of a calling. God
calls each individual to activities in this world and one does
well by faithful obedience to such a calling. After the Reformation, people began to consider that one could find any kind of
work subject to such a divine calling. Therefore, one could
serve the deity not merely in one's field of work, but precisely
through one's field of work. If that meant to use one's talents
to acquire gain, so be it. One was to be the dutiful steward of
one's talents. (2) The idea of the unmediated individual. Each
person is responsible to the deity directly. Replacing the
model of an organic society was the model of private enterprise
in religion, in society and, afortiori, in business. People no
longer accepted the power of the state or church to tell them
what business they could or could not do. The Puritans especially emphasized the shift from state or church intervention to
individualistic self-reliance and non-interference by government.
A person was limited only by one's own capabilities and initiative.

In America, this "Protestant Ethic" translated into an intrinsic ethical rationale for efficiency and profits in business.[1] The new nation grew with a standard of economic reward
incentives for personal effort and astuteness. "Hard work pays
off in income and social status." Benjamin Franklin more than
anyone articulated this ethos for Americans.
   "Remember that time is money."
   "God helps them that help themselves."
   "Early to bed and early to rise,
    Makes a man healthy, wealthy, and wise."

"Plough deep while sluggards sleep."
"Never leave that till tomorrow which you can do today."
We must not judge Franklin's articulation of economic virtues
to express inversion of "virtue as the means to business success. True, honesty is useful because it assures credit; and
also useful are punctuality, industry, frugality. These are
business virtues. And while Franklin admits that even the appearance of such virtues would suffice for the desired reaction
of others, he assumed, as did most other early Americans, that
the basis of economic relationships was "a fair exchange for
quality goods and services." He would concur with Washington
(who himself echoed Cervantes) that "Honesty is the best
policy."

Nor can we judge that Franklin's articulations held a
hidden public utilitarianism ("such business virtue is good for
society"). The American business virtue expressed by Franklin
was an ethical duty, and any infraction of its rules would be
an infraction of one's ethical duty. This duty directed how
to use one's time. One used one's time to make money legally.
This effort itself was virtue. And unwillingness to work was
a sign of a lack of virtue (and a lack of grace).[2]

Justice here is the distribution to each according to
each's performance of one's duty. This self-reliance emphasis
corresponded well with the social presupposition of individual
liberty and a fair distribution of opportunity in the new land.

What made this business spirit unique was not the effort to
make money. As Max Weber notes, the auri sacra fames was not
peculiar to bourgeois capitalism.[3] What was new was the change
in attitude. Earlier, even the persons in business themselves
considered their activities as either non-moral or even immoral
and to be somehow reconciled before death. But with the change
wherein business and money-making could be an ethical duty in
itself, there was now an intrinsic ethical justification for
efficient business practices. This justification functioned
not only among persons in business, but also within the ethic
dominant in society well into the twentieth century. It was
also very compatible with Laissez-Faire capitalism in the
classical mode.

This compatibility is the more surprising when we note
that, for Adam Smith, the ethical justification for free choice
business enterprise (laissez-faire capitalism) was in terms of
the utilitarian good of society, and not individual duty. Moreover, for Smith, this societal justification was not, or at
least need not be, the motive for economic activity. Rather,
the motive was self-interest in a free exchange relationship.

He (the businessperson)... neither intends to promote the
public interest, nor knows how much he is promoting it.

...(B)y directing that industry in such a manner as its
produce may be of the greatest value, he intends only his
own gain, and he is in this, as in many other cases, led
by an invisible hand to promote an end which was no part
of his intention. By pursuing his own interest he fre-
quently promotes that of the society more effectually than
when he really intends to promote it.[4]

Smith's thesis on the relation of business to the good of society
was that the pursuit of economic self-interest in the free market was the best system to achieve those results from the business enterprise which would be the best possible contribution in
terms of economic consequences for any society. The system would
guide the efficient use of all scarce resources in a society in
such manner as to produce the consequences which the real needs
of the people in society would select. Justice would be "to
each according to one's choice and one's efficiency."

With this attitude, people could live in society and embrace
individual self-interest in economic exchange. The only requisite was adherence to fair rules of the exchange, not common purposes of the individuals engaged in the exchange.[5] The liberty
element in self-interest, it should be noted, is important but
secondary. F. A. Hayek writes: "The important point...is that
(this system) reconciles different knowledge and different purposes which, whether the individuals be selfish or not, will
greatly differ from one person to another. It is because in the
market order men...will further the aims of many others, most of
whom they will never know, that it is as an overall order so superior to any deliberate organization."[6]

There is one important presupposition here that remains unexamined. Profit seeking through efficiency alone was ethically
justified in terms of producing items that corresponded to the
needs of the people. But no one ever proved that needs expressed
through exchanges were the same as the "real" needs of people.

However, there is some measure of consequential justification for the Smithian thesis from its historical results. Free
enterprise claims justification because it claims to make the
most efficient use of material and human economic resources to
create the greatest opportunities for free choice, for personal
development and for material well-being for the greatest num-
bers. And the present standard of living for those countries
that have had significant measure of free enterprise cannot be
ignored in its support. Also, the psychological importance of
initiative in the self-appreciation of conscious dignity continues to gain significance with its correlation to happiness.

Surprisingly, there is one point of clash between the
"Protestant Ethic" and the "Free Enterprise Ethic" that cannot
be overlooked: the former weighs heavily the subjective effort,

the latter weighs heavily the objective efficiency. In other
words, not all who do their duty to the best of their abilities
succeed. By honest effort, one becomes respectable. But one
need not become rich. The market keeps wiping out the inefficient and failure is as much a part of economic life as is success. To handle this fact, a third important element in the
business ethics of the American heritage was needed: the ethics
of having losers in business competition.

Many theories contributed here, as well as some intuitive
feelings of fairness. "Social Darwinism" gave an explanation
in that it offered a rationale for letting competition weed out
losers. Herbert Spencer, especially, applied the "natural selection" principle from Darwin to human society. This principle maintained that there is a kind of "natural law" whereby
those who are best adapted to survive in a given environment
actually do survive and reproduce. Something analogous to a
"selection" goes on, even though there is no "selector." In a
utilitarian mode of verification, therefore, one could argue
that, if one left the competitive market alone, those who did
more for the total societal enterprise would thrive, while those
who did not do as well, no matter their effort, would fail.[7]

Social Darwinism was not completely accepted by the American psyche. Mitigating Social Darwinism in practice was the
Protestant theory of stewardship or "trust." Those who succeeded were considered endowed with unique gifts given to them
from the start as a sort of trust. Certainly each was to employ
such gifts in each's assigned duties. But those who succeeded
and were objectively rewarded economically were expected in turn
to do actions for the benefit of those who, not by their own
fault, did not yet succeed. This "social dimension" of business
enterprise was not simple charity (albeit it may have been named
such). It was a trust, and it was just as much a duty of the
successful to find ways to redistribute their economic success
for the benefit of the lesser fortunate of society as it was to
employ their economic skills in business itself.

There was also another aspect, a feeling, that could explain
the American acceptance of competition. This aspect actually is
more compatible with the American spirit of freedom, fairness,
and putting all assertions to the test. Fair competition was
there to prove what was best (fit), and it always was a hard
test if it was truly fair, and a test anyone was free to avoid.
But it was the only possible real test. Human beings can gain
certainty about something in no other way than by putting things
to the test of experience in competition with alternatives.
This spirit was important in America, for it went with the general conviction that, in all but a few religious matters, human
understanding has very narrow bounds, and so it is better not to
trust authority on a matter without testing. This seems part of
the heritage from David Hume which was influential in the Amer-

ican spirit and the American Constitution.[8]

Many have explored why this combination from the American past, even though still relatively strong among older persons in business, is no longer dominant in society. Both historical and psychological factors have changed the milieu and there are disputes which grew out of which. So let me simply enumerate a few of these factors. Historically, the great depression of the 1930's destroyed the proposition that there is a connection between hard work, thrift, and the benefits distributed in the economic society. Legally and legislatively the government became encouraged and expected to take a much more active role in the nation's economy. Also with the advent of large corporations with power to control some market factors, people no longer think that the economic market can be self-regulating.[9]

Psychologically, many new dimensions of social life have become more clearly articulated in the attention of people. There are new ideals of "rights" and "equality," ideals in themselves often vague and arguable, but indicative as phenomena of a new societal model. There are questions on the psychological impact on society of an economic model for relationships based on exchange between self-interested persons.

Some find also a fundamental change in people's attitudes toward work itself. Others do not see this change in the same way. For instance, they disagree that we today have a return to the medieval preferences for less work and less difficulty in lieu of more pay and more effort. Rather, many see today a situation with a "rising threshold of job acceptability" (e.g., Robert Heilbroner), that is, not so much a distaste for work and effort as a new and higher estimation of what constitutes a "decent job" befitting the "dignity" of the worker.

Also some find a decline in willingness to put forth effort toward quality. This decline some see as an echo of a change in how people experience satisfaction, in how they measure success. As analyzed by Richard M. Huber, our times with mass production have changed the primary impetus of business from that of building to that of selling (getting others to take goods beyond their real needs or raising their real needs to respond to what business can now produce).[10] In an era of building, quality and effort at work are essential in the conscious evaluation of "success." In an era of selling, they need not be.

These and other factors have put to the question the formerly accepted ethical rationale of business in America.

CHAPTER   TWO

BRIEF REVIEW OF PRINCIPLES   FROM
ETHICAL THEORY

From the look in Chapter One at the former ethical atmosphere for business in America, we might notice two foci:

(1) the personal ethic of character which stressed liberty,
self-reliance, and which was based on the feeling of the unique
dignity of each individual; and
(2) the social ethic of utility which stressed the kinds of
actions and practices which would benefit society.

These two foci make for an unstable ethic, even though it
took some time for this instability to become apparent in our
American consciousness. However, neither the delay nor our
eventual cognizance is proof that the instability itself can be
overcome. We have no apriori assurance that any operative ethic
can avoid instability, for our world is complex and dynamic, and
any action could have ramifications of various kinds and evaluations. To phrase this in ethically technical terms: human
action situations often involve conflicts of rights. To phrase
it in the technical terms of economics or mathematics: one must
make tradeoffs when two or more independent functions cannot be
maximized simultaneously.

Consequently, one need not expect unanimity among ethicians
on any ethical problem in business. To see this more clearly,
we might make broad classifications of ethical perspectives.
Most ethical principles can be grouped into four major classifications: act utilitarianism; rule utilitarianism; absolute deontology; and anchor deontology. All four of these have defenders.
And all four are theoretical efforts to explain not only "why is
this action right or wrong," but also "how does one know this."

I. The Spectrum in Theoretical Ethics

To introduce these four classes, we might recall some opin-
ions expressed concerning acts of civil disobedience. Are such
acts good or bad ethically? Some would say such acts are good
because they are means to social progress. Others say such acts
are bad because they bring about disrespect for the law. Both of
these use the same method of verification: an appeal to the consequences in society. This method of verification falls under
the general heading of Utilitarianism (or sometimes Consequen-
tialism). Another group might argue that such acts were bad because a citizen has a duty to obey the law simply because one is

11

a citizen. This method of verification appeals to some intrinsic meaning in the act and refers the act, not to consequences, but to some atemporal structure. This method of verification falls under the general heading of Deontology. Both Utilitarianism and Deontology divide into two still very broad subclasses, and the four make up the following spectrum of positions.

((A))Act Utilitarianism. This set of ethical principles works to verify the ethics of individual acts. Act utilitarians judge each act right or wrong on the consequences of that act alone, in comparison with the consequences of alternatives, in respect to a value affected by the consequences. The formal principle is: choose that which promises the best for the value. Since the operative value itself is not specified, act utilitarians differ as to what value is to be singled out for maximization (e.g., pleasure; societal development; equal satisfaction of preferences; satisfaction of rationally chosen interests; etc). The act is given a "utility" ranking (either cardinal, with a number designating positive units of utility, or ordinal, with a comparative adjective such as "more,""less,""first,""second").

There are some problems with act utilitarianism. (a)What kinds of values does the individual desire to enhance and should one desire these values? (b)How does one measure utility? An individual can make simple preference judgments allowing for some indifference among some groups of alternatives (the indifference curves). But what of acts or social practices that affect others? Kenneth Arrow argues that (1)a satisfactory aggregation procedure using ordinal preferences and some form of voting does not exist, and (2)even if one did exist, such would fail to take into account the intensity in the individuals and in the group. Sometimes, a minority can feel more intensely about an issue than a majority. Finally, (c)what criteria would determine what alternatives are available? We often assume that our alternatives are intuitively obvious. Yet at best we only have probable knowledge of the set of relevant consequences for our actions.

To avoid the chaos and burden of calculation at each decision time, which would make society impossible and life too turbulent, many prefer the position of Rule Utilitarianism.

((B))Rule Utilitarianism. This set of ethical principles works also to verify the ethics of individual acts. But it distinguishes the ethical relation to a rule in society (e.g., keeping one's contract) of an act, and the evaluation of the rule itself. For the act utilitarian, an act is good, at least not bad, if nobody gets hurt by it. For the rule utilitarian, an act is good if performance of a similar act by all similar agents would produce the best results in society overall (the "what if everyone ...?" approach), or has done so (the "wisdom of the past" approach). The rule itself is evaluated on the consequential good

for society of kinds of actions by similar classes of agents.
The rule functions as a standard by which to evaluate the act
and works deductively: "people should keep their contracts for
the stability of society; I have made a contract; therefore..."

One should notice that both these utilitarian theories are
open to many basic values and can be employed by those who differ on what values anchor their involvement in ethical evaluations in the first place. Both theories concentrate on the question of verification ("how do I know that this act ethically is
good or bad"), but neither resolves the question "why am I involved in ethical evaluation at all," or the question "is this
ethical involvement unavoidable or optional."

((C)) Absolute Deontology. This set of ethical principles works
to verify the ethics of individual acts in terms of the unavoidable meaning to me of acts in reference simply to some atemporal
standard. It is termed "absolute" because it claims the meaning
to me of my ethical actions is absolved of dependence on the consequences of actions. The theory depends on certain elements in
the description of the kinds of actions and claims these elements
are ethically decisive "whatever the consequences." As a result,
the theory has difficulties when conflicts of rights in alternatives entails an unavoidable negation of values. The standard
"It is wrong to kill a human being" has at times forced people
to do or to permit the negation of values they later came to
judge were more important.

((D)) Anchor Deontology. This set of ethical principles works
once again to verify the ethics of individual acts in terms of
the unavoidable meaning to me of acts. But here the unavoidabil-
ity is not in terms of kinds of acts, which here are only presumptive (prima facie) standards, but in terms of some anchor
for value in my life which is not arbitrary in significance.
The theory identifies the anchor for value in terms of the unavoidable respect one acknowledges in reference to the "dignity
of human persons."

With this base, one makes the additional step to judge by
reflection on experience just how certain individual acts or
certain kinds of acts have consequences in relation to this dignity in each person affected. Individual acts or kinds of acts
have meaning derivatively from this unavoidable respect for dignity, and their consequences in relation to this dignity may
change with time and situation. Anchor deontology can employ
not only presumptive standards but also act and rule utilitarianism, as long as it specifies the values to be maximized in
reference to the dignity of persons.

In this work, I employ this anchor deontology, and work with

the "rights" of persons based on such dignity. In order that
one may concretize the notions of dignity and rights, I offer
the following. While there is much argument over some of the
criteria of human dignity, one is not precipitate to identify
some commonly acknowledged elements such as "the conscious capa-
bility to self-order one's actions" and "the felt significance
in one's experiences often due to self-projected goals which, as
lived out, give one joy and satisfaction, or, as frustrated, give
one sadness and dissatisfaction." From this unavoidable respect
for dignity, one may phrase the Fundamental Ethical Principle as
follows: "always act so as to treat others as persons with dignity" (a positive principle), or (a negative principle) "never
act so as to limit this dignity."

From this Fundamental Ethical Principle, one can argue that
here follows certain "rights" that are to be respected in actions
and one can also work toward a derivative principle for guidance
when there are conflicts of rights.

II. Rights, Conflicts of Rights, and the
Principle of Double Effect

When the Fundamental Ethical Principle is stated positively,
"always act so as to treat others as persons with dignity," it
functions as an ideal and usually designates a wide set of alternatives. When the Principle is stated negatively, "never act
so as to limit this dignity," it functions as a limit. One negative expression of the principle is well-known: "never use
another person merely as a means."

This negatively stated principle is ambiguous, for one does
not intuitively grasp the importance of the adverb "merely."
Without the adverb, almost all business transactions would violate the principle. The customer uses the grocer to facilitate
the acquisition of food. The seller uses the buyer to increase
revenues. The driver uses the gasoline station attendent to service the car. We do not consider these uses of others as prima
facie wrong. On the other hand, complaints are often heard that
"the other person just used me,""they just manipulate us for
their own purposes." And there is within these complaints the
suggestion that such actions are wrong. Consequently, one struggles to clarify the principle as one struggles with individual
ethical problems in actual situations. It is in these correlative struggles that there is reciprocal clarification of the importance of the adverb "merely" and the ethical correctness of
individual actions. Concretely, one cannot clarify exactly how
the word "merely" is to be understood for all ethical situations.
However, even at the start, one need not remain entirely on the
empty, formal level.

First, one finds a little assistance from the positive

statement of the Fundamental Ethical Principle. From it one can expand the negative statement to read: "never act so that I debilitate or eliminate the conditions for another to act as a self-ordering person." One needs only a little experience to sense the need of this expansion. For our world is very complex today, and the lines of interactions and interaffecting the lives of one another never separate.

Secondly, we can also circumscribe to some extent the possible ethical boundaries for this interaffecting. As I act in the world, my action affects the physical things and the social and organizational relationships of persons. According to anchor deontology, we can locate guiding boundaries to the legitimacy of this interaffecting. These boundaries are located with the use of the intelligibilities of Rights.

There are four major kinds of rights.

(1) Contract Rights. These rights come from any sort of agreement on the part of those involved and are conditioned by the partial fulfillment of the contract by any of the parties. These contracts may be private and they may be social. Some private contracts are enforceable by societal law, and some social contracts are given expression in society's constitution and subsequent legislation.

(2) Merit Rights. These rights accrue to those who have performed actions which "deserve" some "reward" or who have displayed a characteristic which "deserves" some "reward." That such actions or characteristics do deserve such rewards and what rewards are deserved are questions that can only be answered on the presupposition that there exist "practices" acknowledged by all those involved. All questions with regard to merit rights take as a reference the practice appurtenant which consists in rules which designate the actions, positions, rules and rewards that make up the practice. (For example, sports contests, grading, beauty contests, some religious moralities are practices.)

(3) Positive Rights. These rights arise through legislative and judicial action in a society and are predictions of society's willingness to enforce the claims of its members on one another.

(4) Dignity Rights. These rights belong to persons simply because they are persons in a temporal world. They are the horizon by which the ethician judges the ethics of contract, merit, and positive rights, which are consequently derivative rights.

For this work, permit me to stipulate a description of dignity rights. Dignity rights are the claims made by persons to those kinds of items in general (a) which are necessary for them to live as temporal, limited, self-ordering agents in this world;

(b) which items are vulnerable to the actions of others, be these others individuals, practices, or institutions; and, consequently (c) the claims to which items other persons have intelligibly coercive reasons to respect and order their actions, practices and institutions to acknowledge. For example, one needs a certain amount of information gained by credible communication, one needs a certain amount of material goods, one needs a certain level of self-respect, one needs a certain security because of physical fragility of the human body and the human psyche. Without respect by others for these claims, one could not function as a self-ordering agent in this temporal world. The verification here would consist in an appeal to experience.

If this were a world in which conflicts of rights never arose, the ethical principle stated above would, of course, always function directly. And we would have only to face the question of the accurate delineation of the basic principle. In such a world without conflicts, one could come to ethical decisions simply by asking what rights were at stake, and then act upon the rational judgment that had as its derivative principle:

"The dignity (and derivative) rights of others ought to be supported by one's actions."

However, in this real world of ours, two ever-present structures complicate the moral decisions: (1) finite in space and time, whenever I do an act A, there is not the possibility at the same time of doing act B; and (2) with temporal successiveness, when I do act A, I change the conditions so that act B can never again be a real possibility exactly in the same way. Now, if act B involves a rational claim because of the dignity or merit of another person, I, by doing act A, insofar forth negate that right of the other person.

The ethical problem whenever there is a situation where I must do either act A or act B, and each involves a right, is called a "conflict of rights." And the ethical problem in a conflict of rights (dignity and/or derivative) is radical: if each of my options for action involves the negation of the rights of some, how can I act rationally, if it is rational so to order my actions as to respect the rights of all self-orderers. Because there are conflicts of rights, we must suspect that it is not always wrong to act or to have practices which negate some rights of persons. The suspicion, however, must be elaborated into a rational principle. This principle by which the act is to be judged as rational must be consistent with the person's basic ethical principle, even though negative effects with respect to the ethical rights of some are foreseen. The ordinary person speaks of "doing the best one can," or of "making the best of a complex situation."

The Principle of the Double Effect (hereafter: PDE) has been suggested as that rational principle which functions in ethically correct decisions in matters where there is a conflict of rights. The principle is to be distinguished from the Principle of Efficiency (hereafter: PE). The PE is a principle for an action which aims at a value with the accepted exclusion of some persons from this value, which exclusion is brought about by the action itself, even though there is no intelligible principle for the exclusions. The PE, consequently, will not be intelligibly coercive for the thought of all, for another person or group need not find the action beneficial toward individual/group interests and see no reason, beyond physical force or emotional coercion, to acquiesce in it. The PDE, to be different, must disclose that it is intelligibly coercive.

To disclose any such intelligible coerciveness, let me here review the four elements that must function if the PDE ethically controls an action, practice, or institution that negates the rights of human self-orderers.

(1) One who does an action which for ethical rationality appeals to the PDE, acknowledges by the very appeal that the negation of the dignity/derivative rights of self-orderers is germane. If this negation alone were the outcome, obviously the act would be a simple contradiction of the Fundamental Ethical Principle and be judged unethical. Thus, for the PDE to function intelligibly, the agent must in the action assert a right which, as a right of persons, is intelligible and therefore coercive for the thought of all. The action which negates a right must have as its intended outcome the respect for a right that belongs to all persons.

The intelligible content of this first element of the PDE is this: the action must involve two distinct rights. And the ethical principle would say that it is right to act so as to respect the right supported. It is irrational to bring about the negation of the right of any person unconnected with some expression of respect for the rights of persons. In other words, there must be at least two effects of the act (or practice) in respect to rights, one of which effects must be the positive affirmation of respect for the rights of persons.

(2) The second requisite element of the PDE is meant to handle the question: when there is a conflict of rights, on what basis does one decide which right to assert? On what principle can one rationally argue that this person or group must bear the onus of the dilemma in a conflict of rights? (Recall: a rational principle for ethical action is one by which one can express in action a respect for the dignity of persons.)

For the ethician, there is here not a question of private

emotion or aristocentric preference. And if there is no rational principle by which the conflict of rights dilemma can be resolved, then the ethician can only conclude that the PE functions. For the only articulable principle of the action ("it is
right to assert a right for persons by an action that negates a
right for some persons") precisely is self-contradicted in the
performance. The principle for the action would assert the primary value of self-ordering persons, and limit the scope of this
respect. In no intelligible way would the act show that one has
fundamental respect for persons.

The Fundamental Ethical Principle's negative form can now
be sharply described. If the action of P_1 justifies itself by
appeal to R_1, which is the right claimed, yet the action of P_1
itself effects the limitation of P_2 from R_1, then the action of
P_1 asserts that P_2 is not a person, but a thing to be used,
a "means" only.

The only way to avoid the irrational limitation of the PE,
which denies a right to a person while at the same time affirms
a right to a person, is to uncover another right that is also
involved, a right that also belongs to all persons, and that can
base an intelligible principle for the act of the agent, which
act affirms a right for all persons, including the one who has
a right negated by the act.

This second right could support a principle for an act
which does negate a right but an act which still shows rational
respect for persons without any irrational limit to the respect.

Many presuppositions would be necessary for such a solution.
Certainly involved would be (a) that there is such a thing as a
hierarchy of rights (we often say, "It was more important that I
do that..."); and (b) that the negation of a lower right does
not entail a limit on the universality of the affirmation of the
higher right.

Which rights in fact are higher is a question out of place
here, but one consequence of the PDE function is this: one should
not apriori consider any right as an absolute right, that is, a
right to be affirmed in all situations. However, the right is
always presumptively decisive, and the burden of proof lies on
the one who would negate that there is a higher right at stake
in the conflict of rights.

(3) The third requisite element of the PDE states that the

agent who performs the act made ethically rational by the principle is able to combine two attitudes in consciousness: (a) psychologically one of course must intend whatever is necessary to affirm the right supported; but (b) ethically one is not complacent with the negation of right also resultant. This latter negation of a right is, as foreseen in consciousness, psychologically intended. It would be word-games to deny this. But there is an intelligible basis to the claim that one can psychologically intend the negation of the right and still not want it. The one who acts does not want the negation of the right which is foreseen because one continues to acknowledge the right involved to be a right of persons. Also, the right affirmed by the action itself gains its ethical rationality insofar as it is the affirmation of a right that, in principle, is a right of all persons.

This third element, of course, is a corollary to the second. Only if there is the reality of the higher right uncovered in the discussion of the second requisite element can one support the claim that the respect for persons is upheld without limit even as one negates a right. Yet this third requisite element decisively eliminates the possibility of acting ethically unless one continuously acknowledges the rights of all persons. The sign of this continuous acknowledgment will be the sensitivity to the fourth requisite element.

(4) There must be proportionality, both in the sense of what is done intentionally for the sake of the intended outcome, and in the sense of the outcome intended in relation to the negation of rights permitted.

If the analysis of the first three requisites for the PDE holds, this fourth requisite becomes rather self-explanatory. For we have uncovered why the proportionality must be observed in order that the PDE is to function as a rational principle for action in conflicts of rights. (a) If one has a rational respect for persons as self-orderers; and (b) if one acknowledges that rights are claims by persons that intelligibly coerce actions; then (c) one will constantly take care that encroachment upon rights by one's actions will take place only insofar as is necessary for the expression of higher, conflicting rights.

The PDE is used today by many to handle ethical problems, even though most people do not identify it by name. It is a solid principle that rationally functions in the resolution of conflicts of rights. But it is this solid principle if, and only if, the above analysis, or some such analysis, makes the PDE itself intelligible in subordination to the Fundamental Ethical Principle.

CHAPTER   THREE

HORIZONS AND THE INSTITUTION OF BUSINESS

I have already suggested the connection between ethics and any person's experience of meaningfulness. I will now develop this connection as a way to enter the ethics of business itself. In the Introduction, I employed the metaphor of "horizon." By this metaphor one tries to indicate, among other things, the possible variations for a person's immediate attention and interpretation in a situation in the world. Correlative to actual present interests, the person attends to only some elements of the manifold in present conscious experience, and understands what is going on accordingly. People often refer to a "standpoint," or a "perspective," words that also are metaphors associated with "horizon."

I. Horizons

At a particular standpoint and against a particular horizon, a person gains meaning and significance for individual actions and events. Broadly defined:

((Def)) <u>Horizon</u>: reference for meaning in actions/events.

Since I find this a useful metaphor, let me expand on its function in the general form of "the meaning-for-me of x." How does the metaphor of "horizon" articulate a factor which functions as I obtain meaning in an action or event? Let us look at some examples.

Two husbands bring home flowers to their wives on the same evening. One wife takes the flowers with care and gives the husband a volcanic kiss. The other wife throws the flowers back at the husband and slams the door on him. A student sits in class daydreaming until the professor inserts as a parenthesis the comment, "This next bit will be on the test Friday."

The raw materials for the experience are empirically available to an observer. But these materials all receive interpretation from the reference for meaning that the one who experiences them has and employs. The combination of the empirical raw materials and the way to interpret them disclose the meaning-for-me of any human experience.

((<u>Conditional and Limited Horizon</u>)) A conditional horizon is a reference for meaning in individual events which is dependent on the condition that one accepts the horizon as functioning. It is conditional because it could be otherwise, if the person "looked at things differently" (i.e., from another standpoint with another horizon). The conditional horizon functions only when the person or persons involved accept and enter into the experiential transaction with the dependent condition. Of course, this need not be a volitional dependence, for it could be functional on the condition that one is born in a certain culture, raised in a certain religion, and so on.

The horizon is called limited when it functions only for one who limits attention for a certain period to events or actions insofar as they relate to a role or to an enterprise one has undertaken. Thus the limit for an horizon for the physical scientist will generally be the "push and pull" of things or chemical interchanges and, more specifically, the same data as interpreted by theories or hypotheses. As long as one acts in the role of physical scientist, one cannot explain anything except in reference to such limited horizons, for nothing else is relevant. To say to the physical scientist, as long as she continues in the conditional and limited horizon of her role as physical scientist, that the car accident will be expensive, has no meaning. The chemist can promise "better living through chemistry," but the chemist has no interpretive horizon, as chemist, by which to explain what or why something is better.

All limited horizons themselves seem to have meaning, for they all come about through the activity of persons. They result from human enterprises. Logically, one could argue that, since these limited horizons themselves have meaning, they must be in turn within broader, less limited horizons for persons.

((Unlimited Horizons)) Some horizons are those reference items from which one draws meaning in actions and events which meaning involves one as a person, and not just in reference to some aspect of one's transactions or to one of the rules one undertakes in transactions. I call this one's unlimited horizon. It is the reference from which one judges the adequacy of one's life. It is unlimited in the sense of "whole" as opposed to "part."

From recent study, we know that such unlimited horizons for individuals can enter into human experience in one of two ways: one either acquires such an horizon, or one "projects" such an horizon for oneself. Let us call the former an "other-directed" unlimited horizon. By the term "other-directed," one implies that the references which function in one's consciousness to achieve meaning-for-the-person are accepted from others and as yet remain unexamined by the individual. Consequently, what is considered significant or important is indirectly told to the person by the psychological influence of others.

We call the latter way to acquire an unlimited horizon a "project." By the term "project," one implies that the free decision of the individual person is not only the cause (the explanation that the horizon functions in consciousness) but the ground (the explanation why the horizon is as it is) of the unlimited horizon.

There is one problem for the ethician in respect both to the "other-directed" and to the "project" unlimited horizons. Both are still conditional, both could be otherwise.

((Unconditional Horizon)) Thus, for the ethician, one more step remains if the ethician has hopes of saying anything about human activities in general. But one must admit that there is dispute on this one more step.

There are many who argue that there is no further horizon, that all horizons are conditional. If this is true, then, I submit, we are restricted to sociological studies of what standards in ethics people actually have, and to management studies of what social institutions factually bring about whatever satisfaction of desire those in social power deem worthy of consolidated effort. For with only conditional horizons that could be otherwise, there is no intelligible principle that could convince in argument that a certain meaning, a certain ethical standard, a certain social product should be aimed at.

As a brief argument in support of an unconditional horizon, we might pose the reflective question whether there is any meaning in taking on an "other-directed" unlimited horizon or a "project" unlimited horizon. Sartre, for one, would respond to our question negatively. For him, the project is the source of all meaning-to-the-person, and this is so basic as to be at the cost of loss of freedom if it were otherwise. I am free only if I am the cause and the ground of my unlimited horizon, of the meaning in my life. But this consciously free project essentially is conditional. I can always freely negate any project I have and thus make meaning-for-me otherwise. For Sartre, the meaning of a project in itself can only be talked about in an equivocal manner, as a logical requirement of the very structure of human consciousness. No one can act at all without an implicit direction ("project"), and so under the prohibition of logical contradiction one must make projects. But there is no meaning for oneself in which project one makes.

Sartre's friend, Albert Camus, objected to Sartre's position. Camus could not accept that it really makes no difference whether or not one is a murderer. For Camus, there were some items, such as innocent children, about whom certain conditions, such as suffering, were important to human ethical experience in a manner that was unavoidable, that is, that could not be otherwise.

This present work, as an anchor deontology, has the dignity of persons as the unavoidable or unconditional horizon for ethical actions. I may describe such an unconditional horizon as follows: "the response to persons that is significant to my consciousness prior to and underlying any human action (including projects) that I freely do."

II. Secondary Horizons

Our lives in society are very diversely interpreted. And these diverse interpretations are not adequately explained by the use of the three kinds of horizons we have studied so far. We must also look at what I call "secondary horizons."

One functions with a secondary horizon when, as one concerns oneself with the ethical interpretation of decisions, one does not employ the Fundamental Ethical Principle alone, but employs in addition or in substitution specific models or specific practices or specific theories as to how to act well in specific dimensions of society. For example, from the combination of the fundamental principle and the investigation of requirements for persons to act well as self-orderers in this temporal world, we could designate among rights of persons such an item as "true information about a particular point of fact in a one-on-one situation." But must one always tell the simple truth about the factual situation whenever one is asked? Even when there is no immediate need by the questioner for information to act well as a self-orderer?

Traditionally the response has been "yes." The argument has been formed as follows. "If the speaker could so act as to tell the truth or not according to the speaker's own judgment whether the seeker truly had an immediate right to the true information, then no seeker would know when the speaker was telling the truth, for one could never be sure if the speaker judged that there was an immediate right to the information at issue. So the conclusion is that the speaker must always tell the truth because of the intermediate right of the seeker to that atmosphere of truth-telling in a society within which one could assume that one received the truth when one did need it." This right to an atmosphere of truth was derivative from the basic right to receive the truth as needed to act as a self-orderer, derivative because it was necessary to achieve the condition of credible communication, which condition itself is necessary to establish the primary right.

Yet we know that simple candor is not always socially beneficial. And we know that some materially correct statements actually become harmful at times (e.g., when they support false attitudes in hearers; when they contribute to a weakening of important social institutions; or when they violate legitimate

demands of privacy). And in experience people express themselves and receive the expression of others, and judge them as
ethically satisfactory, and yet know that these expressions are
not literally true. This would indicate that kinds of secondary horizons function in human communication, such as "social
oil" phraseology ("She's not here" said on the telephone), or
professional role-playing practices. In our society, secondary
horizons are normally used and judged ethically adequate if one
can legitimately expect that the seeker/hearer should be sophisticated enough to be able to anticipate a given form of response
and be able to translate accordingly.

Other kinds of secondary horizons appear in the use of specific models or practices or "myths" to direct one how to act
well in specific dimensions of society. The model of the professional scientist or engineer; the specific practice of business or sports competition come to mind at once. As for myths,
the ideal of earning one's own way stands out in our culture.
(Recall: myth does not mean "unreal" or "fictitious." Myth has
a technical sense to describe the stories, symbols, attitudes,
or ideals that a culture tells itself in order to articulate
those values and energies which cannot be rationally articulated
at a given stage of culture.)

All secondary horizons act as a second stage to fill out
the rather formal imperative of the Fundamental Ethical Principle. These secondary horizons are cultural contributions which
direct our efforts as we strive to live out in our complex world
of relationships our lives with other persons. Since we are to
concentrate in this work on business and ethics, let us take a
casual look at three myths that have functioned as secondary horizons in the domain of earning a living.

III. Three Cultural Myths in Business

There is no call here to be complete in listing the cultural myths that one can discover in our attitudes concerning that
part of our lives indicated by the general phrase "earning a living" or the more comprehensive term "the business institution."
All we wish to do here is to make explicit some of the myths that
function in our consciousness as referents for interpretation of
the meaning of our actions in this area.

(A) Success. We have never as a people completely resolved our
fascination with what William James long ago titled "the bitch
goddess Success." The American psyche wants as its hero the one
who succeeds, who wins. Yet the same psyche detests the winner
and wants the winner humbled (self-humbled satisfies at times)
or even toppled. American culture both affirms and denies that
success is a supreme public value. (I here ignore the very recent fascination with the "being Number One is everything" craze,

which not only is too young to evaluate, but at best is an aberration.)

Perhaps the success myth took roots in the conviction that America is the land of opportunity. Insofar as it is, to fail in America is a particularly bitter humiliation which cannot be blamed on external forces. In a particularly interesting essay, "The Gangster as Tragic Hero," Robert Warshow suggests that our ambivalence toward success is central to the American movie gangster of the thirties and the forties.

The gangster hero was doomed, not because his method to achieve success was wrong according to the law (which it was), or because his method toward success was irrational (which it was not---the gangster carried on very rationally with definite goals and techniques, a perfect execution of MBO). The gangster was doomed because he was under obligation to succeed in the modern urban context. The film and its audience both agreed that, in human life, a person is a being with the possibilities of success or failure, and with the demand to emerge from the crowd in the city or else remain nothing. "On that basis the necessity of the action is established, and it progresses by inalterable paths to the point where the gangster lies dead and the principle has been modified: there is really only one possibility---failure."[1]

The gangster was a tragic hero of the society of opportunity and also its victim. The ambiguity of economic success remorselessly works things out. "In the deeper layers of the modern consciousness, all means are unlawful, every attempt to succeed is an act of aggression, leaving one alone and guilty and defenseless among enemies. . . . This is our intolerable dilemma: that failure is a kind of death and success is evil and dangerous. . . . The effect of the gangster film is to embody this dilemma in the person of the gangster and resolve it by his death."[2]

In the last few decades, there has been some apparent modification of the success myth. We have not eradicated it, but we have the concepts. The Protestant Ethic conceived and measured success in terms that, if not simply of material accumulation, were at least definable as some type of getting ahead in material possessions. Dale Tamowieski, in The Changing Success Ethic, speaks of the evidence we have today that many now think of success in terms of "greater job satisfaction" or "achievements in non-career goals."[3] Richard M. Huber, in The American Idea of Success, speaks of the change from building to selling as the model, and argues that today we stress character less and personality more.[4]

There is a further concretization of the success myth that

must be mentioned: status. Status can be described as one's
place in that stratification in society determined by the relation one has with those organizations important within the technologically industrial society. One's position in organizations
correlates with the range in which one has the power effectively
to do something. Since status comes by relation to organizations, the determination works both ways. The individual determines within the organizational structures one's own life and
the lives of others in proportion to one's status. But the organizational structures in turn determine the self-identifica-
tion of the individual (and the family)---who one is to oneself
and to others. One who gains identity by this status is subject
to the fate and to the power of the various organizations themselves. And so this success is also ambiguous.

(B) Work. A second myth which functions as a secondary horizon
in our business culture concerns the basic attitudes toward work.
I noted at the end of Chapter One some recent modifications of
this myth. For our purposes here it is only important to keep
in mind some cultural aprioris about work that still are operative. The myth of work teaches: that work builds character;
that work keeps one from mischief; that when everybody works the
economy is stable and this stability is a prime social value;
that time is valuable itself and so there is an ethical demand
that all people use time to produce by work something of "value";
that no one deserves what one has not earned by work, or, at
least, that only one willing to work deserves to share in the
general store of social goods.

There are several facets to this myth. It states apriori
certain things about the relations (a)between individuals and
their capabilities to use non-working time well; (b)between individuals and their fear of having nothing to do that "has to be
done"; (c)between a person's engagement in, or willingness to
engage in, work that results in a material product, and that person's right to a decent material standard of living.

(C) Self-Interest. This myth is central to the rationality of
laissez-faire economics, but it covers many meanings and it is
not often clear which meaning one uses. Let me explain. Formally, the myth expresses that one's prime motivation is "utility
maximization." That is, the "self" desires maximum utility satisfaction. (This myth that the person is best understood as a
package of desires contrasts with the Aristotelian model which
we look at in Chapter Six.) The variants enter with the differences in (a)what values enter into the utility complex; and (b)
what is felt as the self. There are three possible variants of
the latter.

Self-interest I: the individual aims at utility maximization that
factually is private and independent of the utility enjoyed by

any other person (narcissistic self-interest).

Self-interest II: the individual aims at utility maximization that includes the difference between the individual's own satisfaction and that of others. One will accept fewer goods so long as others receive less also (envious self-interest).

Self-interest III: the individual aims at utility maximization that includes to some degree the well-being of at least some others (expanding self-interest). Writers such as David Hume and William James explored how one can so identify oneself with others that the fortunes of these others bring a rise or fall in one's own utility. The interests of these others are also "mine" in a way that gives meaning to my acts not reducible to self-interest I.[5]

IV. The Subsystem that is Business

Since we will study in this work the ethics that pertain to the business dimension of society, I will treat that secondary horizon for the interpretation of meaning and acting well that is the institution of business in our culture. To set this, I here introduce some useful terms.

((Def)) _Practice_: Any association of definitely patterned human behavior wherein the description and meaning of the kinds of behavior involved and the kinds of expectations involved are dependent upon those rules which define the practice.[6]

An example may clarify this. The physical actions of those who engage in a baseball game are described and names and given significance only as long as the practice of baseball functions. One can only strike out, steal a base, hit a home run in a game of baseball. The practice determines the rationality of the actions within it. The rationality of the practice itself always is in reference to something external to the practice.

((Def)) _Institution_: "A public system of rules which defines offices and positions with their rights and duties, powers and immunities, and the like. These rules specify certain forms of action as permissible, others as forbidden; and they provide for certain penalties and defenses, and so on, when violations occur."[7]

John Rawls, who calls institutions "social practices," writes that an institution exists in a society "when the actions specified by it are regularly carried out in accordance with a public understanding that the system of rules defining the institution is to be followed."[8]

Society as a whole system functions as some sort of loose unity. It has rules which define actions, etc. But also within a society there are subsystems which are institutions. For example, there are the institutions of government and of business. And these institutions have their rules which define actions, etc. Thus we may speak of the "secondary horizon" of the business institution, or more properly, of the "secondary horizon" that is the business institution. We noted earlier that while the making and the executing of decisions in a business firm take place within business's own interpretive horizon, these decisions also take place within the more comprehensive horizon of rights of persons in a society.

As a way to initiate exploration of this relation, let us look at ideas on the rights and purposes of business. To put this in terms just introduced, we can ask: where do the rules come from for the institution of business and how does the institution gain rationality for itself. For government the answers are: it gains its subsystem rationality from principles expressed in the Preamble to the Constitution, and the body of the Constitution sets down structures and procedures by which the intitution of government produces the rules for itself.

The rights involved in the actions of those within the business institution have two foundations: "the right of free association" that obtains for all persons and "the right to act within a well-ordered society as an approved segment." The former is a dignity right expressed also in the Constitution and is called an "inherence" right. The latter is a merit right based on the practice of "concession" by a different, higher societal institution. There is thus a hybrid foundation for the rights involved in business. These two rights which ground the institution of business correspond with two theories on Corporations in Business: the inherence theory and the concession theory.[9] Let us look at these more closely.

The "right of free association" is the right in a free society of persons voluntarily to band together to carry out their own private purposes. With this dignity-contract right, those in business may utilize their resources as they see fit subject only to the limit of negative effects on others. Both from the PDE and from the custom of American liberty, to assert any of my rights is to assume and to assert a respect for a system of these same rights as belonging to all. There is thus an inherent right of persons to engage in enterprise in business. The persons in business are thus the self-ordering source of the rules of the institution of business. And all these rules are in their control in this free association. This may be designated as an expression of the rational principle of subsidiarity. The "principle of subsidiarity" claims that it is irrational to assign to a larger or to a higher societal function that which can be per-

formed successfully by smaller and lower societal functions.
This principle has two arguments. The freedom and dignity of
individuals, to be exercised and appreciated by the individuals,
requires purposes and efforts by themselves and such would be
undermined by absorption by higher functions. Also, each more
comprehensive societal group is designed to be a help to the
lesser groups within it only as needed.

The "right to act within a well-ordered society as an approved segment" corresponds to the concession theory of business
corporations. The reasoning here is, since the business activities produce and distribute the material goods and services
needed by all members in society, the institution is subsidiary
to the members of society in the total complex of their human
purposes in the society. The argument says: the more general
and higher values prevail over the strictly economic values
which latter are values in the "necessary conditions" for human
living, but are not accepted as the highest values in human living. According to this "concession" aspect, the rules in business are subject to the approval of government, which is the institution whose specific function is the public good as a whole.
The institution of business in this horizon is subject to control from outside for the sake of the public good.

There may be a way to reconcile these apparently divergent
rights and theories. Since the freedom of association is based
on dignity of persons, and since the exercise of dignity at all
demands a certain minimum level of economic well-being, then it
seems that, until this minimum is achieved on a reliable basis,
the claim of the entire society upon the business institution
must be primary (on the principle of the goal of social cooperation). But thereafter the subsidiarity principle and free association would seem to be dominant.

Since the rights involved (and also U.S. positive law) make
the institution a hybrid, one would suspect there would also be
a hybrid answer to the question of the purpose of business activity. From the horizon of business as a subsystem, some suggest
that the purpose is to provide the goods and render the services
for the well-being of all in the social cooperation process.
Some suggest that it is not really production here, but freedom
that is the purpose.[10]

But what of the purpose from the horizon of business itself?
Some today still argue that it is profits. Peter Drucker says
this answer is not only false, but it is irrelevant and harmful.[11] Certainly, profit and profitability are crucial in business, but profit maximization (buying cheap and selling dear)
does not explain anything. True, the purpose of profits may explain why some individual gets into a certain line of business.
That is, making money may be the "incentive" for an individual.

But it does not explain what a business does when it operates or
how it should operate or why it does this particular set of activities. Perhaps there is not one specific answer that is the
right one for the question, for the answer is always a decision
by a particular firm and the decision need not forever be valid.
Drucker argues that the purpose of business is "to create a customer."[12] The customer, in turn, determines what a business is,
as the customer acts in response to what the customer considers
a value or, at least, feels is a value area.

V. A Comment on Profits

Profits serve four functions in business: (1) the need for
capital to cover the costs in operations; (2) the need to reduce
the costs of capital, that is, the costs to obtain capital if
there are too few profits; (3) the quantitative measure of effectiveness needed as a guide to make decisions; and (4) the reward
for risks in enterprise, that is, the need for incentives for
promoters and for managers.

These functions give the reasonable explanation for profits.
Without them, the "profit motive" would be itself absolute and
would open to use any activity that paid off. Thus, potentially,
the profit motive would accept a violation of rights.

A further step still remains. After one has established
that profits are reasonable in business, one must still establish that specific individuals have a right to profits, and to
specific profits. I concentrate here on the right to profits
of managers and the right to profits of stockholders.

(MANAGERIAL RETURNS) The manager contributes experience and expertise toward the purpose of the corporation, benefiting both
the corporation and the social order. The manager's decisions
are valuable in reference to the calculation of risks and the
sensitivity to opportunities. To get and to keep qualified managers is so important for the corporation and for society that
the use of incentives cannot rationally be ignored. For these
three reasons, managerial returns are part of the rules of the
institution. One thus can argue that a manager has a merit right
to share in the business profits, which merit right usually is
made explicit by contract.

Just how much is a manager entitled to? According to the
business as subsystem horizon, the answer is "in proportion to
contribution"; according to the business system horizon, the answer is "in terms of the price in the market for managers." However, because of the practical difficulties in the concrete to
determine the exact contribution of any manager, actual salaries
are set in contracts, extras and perquisites, more or less according to the managerial market alone.

Nevertheless, one could make an argument for guidelines to a limit. To do so, one distinguishes between rational incentives and surplus incentives. The rational incentive is the amount that is the minimum necessary to gain and keep an individual in a current line of activity.[13] Involved here, for higher management, is the status function. After a certain level of income, the manager is more sensitive to peer status than to the purchase power of income. In a sense this involves a surplus incentive and in a sense it does not. However, it does raise an ethical problem. Even if one were to argue that status is part of the normal incentive package, people in society judge that the recipient manager does not deserve (merit) the extremely high salary, and this gives the appearance of an unequal income distribution not based on merit.[14] This fosters dissatisfaction and is harmful to the social order.

(STOCKHOLDER RETURNS) Money capital by stockholders makes a necessary contribution to the individual corporation and thereby also to the total social order. By the rules within the institution of business itself, the stockholder rationally merits (1)the return of the money; and (2)as a minimum incentive, a fair market charge for the use of the money. Moreover, as a contribution to the social order, invested capital, according to the rules of business, merits the surplus remaining after fair handling of all explicit costs and, if applicable, after all costs.

The major ethical question arises in reference to the incentive return which is beyond the minimum when it is considered under the horizon of business as a subsystem. Here one must reflect on the notion of "fair" profits. In the total social system, fair profits would be those which supported, or at least did not obviously do harm to the development of the economic dimension of the standard of living for people in society. The principle here is the principle of rational social cooperation.

This principle is a presupposition of a free enterprise principle, which is thereby subordinate to it, since free enterprise presupposes a basic social structure that is mutually advantageous (not necessarily equally advantageous). According to John Rawls, the rule of "rational social cooperation" is "The intuitive idea...that the social order is not to establish and secure the more attractive prospects of those better off unless doing so is (somehow) to the advantage of those less fortunate.[15]

Under this principle, "unusual profits" (say above 10 percent) are a matter of controversy, both in terms of facts (the general public often has a very false concept of how much profits a corporation makes), and in terms of theories as to the effect of such profits on the social good. Some, such as those who follow Keynes, generally oppose high-profit levels on the grounds that they lead inevitably to strong downward business trends, since a mature economy does not need more substantial investment and idle savings precipitate a depression. Others argue that there is a constant need for economic expansion as well as a need for a high profit incentive to secure the necessary investment. Furthermore, as it stands, the controvery remains abstracted from other factors, such as taxes and governmental monetary and fiscal policies, and the status of competition in the field.

As mentioned earlier, the classical rationality for the business institution itself was the utilitarian argument that, when there is freedom for economic values in the market, then maximum human benefits result because goods and services will be produced and allocated efficiently. Even in the classical argument, a company's profits were not its purpose, but its condition of survival. As long as a society was faced with incessant problems of plain economic survival, business did contribute simply and directly to the well-ordered society by its economic activities. People judged that good practices within the business horizon in themselves effected the requisite social benefits from business as an institution. Quality, efficiency and stability in use of resources satisfied the expectations of the society.

In our day, society does not seem satisfied simply with economic results from business. We have changed in respect to the kinds of outputs into society from business we emphasize, and we have changed or are changing in respect to the distribution of these business outputs. Today we call for social benefits affected by, but heretofore not attended to, the operations of business corporations. And today we question just how those in society are to share in the multiple benefits of the business institution. There is a dispute whether these results are to be judged good as long as they are achieved by a fair procedure, or are to be judged good in reference to some standard external to the procedure itself.

This question belongs to the matter of distributive justice, to which we now turn.

CHAPTER   FOUR

DISTRIBUTIVE   JUSTICE

One of the necessary conditions for a collection of human
individuals to become a society is that these individuals share
certain ethical convictions. I stipulate this here on the authority of philosophers from Plato through Hume down to H. L. A.
Hart. These convictions circumscribe the fundamental social
contract or, if one prefers, they pragmatically circumscribe the
fundamental expectations in the public atmosphere. I prefer the
use of the phrase "social contract" and I recommend it as the
expression of some rational theory of justice that has principles of social cooperation that are intrinsically significant to
the dignity of human persons. For a theory of justice, I would
not find suitable the notion of social contract in terms of an
historically imaginative contract. Nor would I accept a contract
model that was "causal," using fear and need only, wherein the
rationality involved would be extrinsic to the characteristic
whereby persons rate ethical respect. A "causal contract" could
base principles for social cooperation only on the value of the
consequences of such cooperation and not for any human good involved in the agreement to the principles itself. In contrast,
by a justicized social contract I indicate one that has intrinsic expression of the dignity of persons, that is, one wherein
principles of cooperation are in themselves, as well as in their
consequences, reasonably consonant with thoughtful and free persons. (I here follow the suggestion of William Frankena that we
use "justicize" to indicate that the principle that makes rational some action, practice, or institution, comes from or is
part of a theory of justice. The term "justicize" is thus more
specific as to the kind of principle that makes something rational than is the more common term "justify.")

Consequently, those societal acts are justicized that are
based upon and are the development of such principles that free
and thoughtful persons could agree to when they could make a
social contract under those conditions wherein all items irrelevant to the basic dignity of the persons, or items based on idiosyncratic presuppositions, were disallowed as significant to
the process of contract decision.

((Def)) Distributive : The cooperation in a society, based on
         Justice   intelligible principles, expressed in
                        the sharing of benefits and burdens of
                        social values that arise because of in-
                        stitutions in that society.

The first appearance of the concept of distributive justice ex-

33

hibits sheer formality and attests to what must still be done
before one can evaluate a social situation or a social dynamic
in its terms. But one can circumscribe what pertains by combining the basic argument for rights and the empirical evidence of
the need to live in harmony in society with the acknowledgment
that society is not simply a congeries but webbed with institutions through which we share the benefits and burdens differently and unequally. By what rational principle(s) can one justicize any actual distribution of benefits and burdens?

The first question to resolve is whether distributive justice is a matter of a process or of an end result, or both. (I
do not include the option of a beginning and a process, such as
included in Robert Nozick's entitlement theory, for any beginning is itself the result of a previous process.[1]) Process distribution is end-independent. That is, the rules for it presuppose those in the process have validly different ends and different hierarchy of ends but they rationally agree that as long
as the process is fair and is followed, the outcome is just.
Justice is determined independently of the end achieved. End
result distribution is end-dependent. The rules for distribution presuppose concrete and specific ends to be achieved by the
process which ends are acknowledged by the rational agreement of
those involved. One judges justice here by comparing the result
with some standard external to the distributional system itself.

I argue that the answer to the question, "process, end result, or both," is: whichever is the most rational in the context. I assume that the persons who compose society are to be
considered self-orderers, anchors for value and unique centers
for the felt significance of things. These persons stand in relation to the existing institutions in society as independent to
dependent. That is, the existing institutions are in principle
justicized if, and only if, meaningfully self-ordering persons
would agree to them in a situation of "fairness for all" as described above.

We are concerned with this question in respect to business.
We note that the benefits and burdens to be distributed by the
business institution are not a static, fixed volume of goods,
but a dynamic, progressive and changing volume. As a help for
the imagination, compare an apple pie and an apple orchard. To
distribute the apple pie, one must decide how to share out an
item which is static and of fixed volume. But to distribute the
apple orchard one must visualize how best to increase the total
number of apples produced and to be distributed. Simply to assert that Person A has more apple trees now than Person B and,
therefore, there is injustice in the distribution is not self-
evidently true. In game theory terms, the distributive justice
of the business institution is not a "zero-sum game" problem, in
which every addition to one player in itself is an equivalent

subtraction from another player.

Therefore, the next problem we have is precisely how to
judge the business institution: a process, an end result, or
both. The most promising method to resolve would be: look at
some suggested maxims for distributive justice and weigh which
one or which ones would appeal to rational agreement in the context specific to business, and then see whether they involve a
process, an end result, or both. These suggested maxims take
the form of rules how a distribution ideally should be guided.

(1) "To each equally (arithmetically)" (=Radical
                                    Egalitarianism[2])

Obviously, this is a maxim more for result than for the process
of the distribution. It is often used in family decisions, but
what of societal economics? Since all those who receive are human and have all consequent respect equally due, some go on to
argue that each in society has as due an arithmetically equal
share of the benefits of societal cooperation, no matter if the
institution in question is a major subsystem. Obviously also,
since not each individual factually could so share, the radical
egalitarian moves usually to the ideal of a group equal sharing
of results. The maxim would thus demand in justice an equal representation of all "significant" groups in all benefits that are
socially significant (quotas on sex, race, ethnic groups, etc).

There are many weaknesses in this maxim and only a few have
considered it even as an ideal. First of all, the maxim involves
a disputable leap from the acknowledged claim of respect due to
all persons to the conclusion that this necessitates an arith-
methic equality in resultant conditions in society. Since many
have and still do hold the first thought and did not and do not
hold the second, there is a prima facie case that the movement
in argument is not self-evident. It seems possible to distinguish equality in certain public rights (equality before the law,
equality in consideration of interests in governmental decisions,
political freedom, etc) and equality in economic benefits. Furthermore, one can distinguish the "floor" of economic benefits
required to remain minimally a political (social) human presence
and the "surplus" shares in an affluent society. Insofar as
there is a "floor" of economic benefits experientially verified
to be requisite for minimal human presence in society, one could
argue by deduction from the Fundamental Ethical Principle that
"a system is unjust if there are more economic shares to satisfy
a claim to the 'floor' economic needs of each member of society,
but the system effects the results that some members are not up
to this 'floor'." Also, it is important to distinguish between
this economic "floor" and the historically rising conscious expectations within a society. It is not a straight deduction
from the fundamental principle that "a system is unjust if there

are more economic shares to satisfy the historically rising expectations for each and every member, but the system effects the
results that some members are not in shares up to their rising
expectations." For one must discern the validity of the rising
expectations.

   With the distinctions, prima facie valid, between public
rights and arithmetic equality in economic results, and between
the "floor" of economic benefits needed for societal presence
and "surplus" shares and shares to meet rising expectations, the
unsubstantiated "leap" from dignity to equality in results cannot help further in the problems of distributive justice.

   Moreover, there is a significant gap in the radical egalitarian maxim itself. Distributive justice was described as
dealing with both the benefits and the burdens of social values
that arise because of institutions. But the result emphasis in
radical egalitarianism ignores the sharing of the burdens. It
especially ignores the sharing in the contribution to the production of social values to be distributed as benefits. The
maxim does not help toward what is just in terms of the contributions of the members of society, nor how to handle the assertion, made in some of the maxims we will see further along, that
there could or should be a connection between sharing the benefits and sharing the burdens.

(2) "From each according to ability, to each according to need"
    (=Straight Socialism[3])

This maxim for distribution has several advantages. It contains
a part to guide the contribution to the production of social values, which part was absent in the Radical Egalitarian maxim.
Also it modifies the part of the maxim on resultant condition.
Intuitively we can see by slight reflection that arithmetic
equality in resultant shares of benefits would be a condition
of useless superfluity for those who, for example, were healthy,
of low metabolism, etc. The needs of persons vary (by age, physical condition, mental abilities, size of family, freely directed
individual or group goals). To have a distributional maxim that
varies accordingly suggests that the putative basis for the Egalitarian position itself (that dignity expresses itself in the
ability to have consciously significant conditions and goals) is
not independent of the variety of human character, desires and
situations.

   What exactly is a need? Formally described, a need exists
when there is something is whose absence a person is harmed in
some manner directly or derivatively connected to human dignity
in the temporally concrete situation. These needs may be dis-
covered empirically, but one must take care to distinguish along
the spectrum between the "floor" needs, the objects that are be-

coming psychological needs due to rising expectations, and the superfluous benefits that are still in all senses luxuries. Some would suggest as a guide something like this: "Whatever all regard as necessary for a decent life becomes a necessity in that society." This could be a guide, but certainly, thanks to the experienced fluctuations of what we have called necessities over the past thirty years, we may safely presume that the tendency is psychologically to identify more items as necessities than prove to be so.

The Straight Socialist maxim also has some weaknesses. The first is in reference to what to do about actual scarcities which involve needs or what to do about actual surplus after all needs are met. The maxim does not guide in reference to the assignment of need priorities in time of scarcity or luxury priorities in time of affluence. Since a perfect meeting of needs and needs alone is a limit result, a rule that only guides in this is rather useless by itself.

The second weakness concerns the identification of those who will judge needs and oversee the distribution. The maxim essentially involves actual and constant political decisions. Human beings are seldom wise enough or consistently good enough to handle such decisions, and it would seem unlikely that such a maxim would be rationally chosen in any social contract if there were any other maxim that promised more assurance.

The third weakness is the absence of any incentive for people to contribute to social products. If each is to receive according to need and this result is unconnected with the contribution according to ability, then some probably will not contribute according to ability. Empirically, we see the connection of some sort of incentive to contribution to social production with a reception of social benefits in every human society. Again, the Straight Socialist maxim has to turn to political determination of how to put people into contributive activities. This once again opens to the problem of the wisdom and goodness of those in political authority. Moreover, it opens to gratuitous differentiation if social rewards begin to vary according to jobs (as they do, for example, in the Soviet Union), since there could be no real individual choice in which job one took.

(3) "To each according to desert connected with some contribution."

This maxim connects contribution and resultant condition. It has many variants, depending on the ranking of different kinds of contribution. And each of the variant rankings (or schedules) would presuppose a social practice wherein there was also included a schedule of rewards. Since each person displays different characteristics or actually performs differently because of

different abilities, development, and motives, according to any
variant of maxim (3), the resultant will always be an inequality
of condition and perhaps a failure in respect to some persons to
meet the "floor" of economic needs. But we should expect this
since such a form concerns the practice and the practice concerns
the process and not directly the end result. Still, it is possible that, given some addendum to cover the "floor" requirement
of the end-result, a maxim in the form that connects contribution to resultant might still be agreed to by persons in a social contract. Let us, therefore, look more closely at some possible varieties with this maxim form.

(3a) "To each according to moral effort in contribution"

We all want the good guys to win and the bad guys to lose, and
we only reluctantly adjust to a story where some semblance of
"moral justice" does not appear. (The bad guys got away once on
Gunsmoke; Perry Mason lost one case.) Unfortunately, we all
tremble at the thought of some one person or the few in government playing the role of moral scorekeeper. David Hume argued
that this drawback eviscerates the (3a) maxim. "But were mankind to execute such a law (which assigned the largest possessions to the most extensive virtue, and gave everyone the power
of doing good according to his inclinations), so great is the
uncertainty of merit, both from its natural obscurity, and from
the self-conceit of every individual, that no determinate rule
of conduct would ever follow from it, and the total dissolution
of society must be the immediate consequence."[4] In our day, F.
A. Hayek concurs with Hume and adds that in a free society one
does not want the material rewards of one's position to depend
upon the recognition of others about the merit one has earned.[5]

(3b) "To each according to any and all non-moral effort in
      contribution"

We strongly feel that hard workers deserve more than loafers.
But the same arguments as those against (3a) apply here also.
Furthermore, there is some reason to suspect in non-moral effort
(as distinct from moral effort) that cultural development does
condition initial abilities and motivation. Thus as we hesitate
to say that one deserves the initial abilities or the cultural
development, we hesitate to say that one simply deserves proportionately to the actual non-moral effort displayed. (Note: both
3a and 3b, albeit with a connection between contribution and received shares, have an emphasis on the end-result.)

(3c) "From each according to one's choice, given one's assets;
to each according to one's contribution to the general economic
well-being, given the market" (=Pure Free Enterprise)

This maxim would handle several of the problems encountered by

the previously suggested maxims. This maxim guides a process in
times of deficiency and surplus, and it provides an incentive
for contribution. It does not need the unreliable judgment of
others. Probably the major weaknesses of Pure Free Enterprise
are the problems of contingency as these affect the "marginal-
ity" of the value of one's productive contribution, which marginal productivity is too chancy for many to rest easy with.[6]

There is not only an impossible task of measurement of contribution in any complex product, there are also elements of
chance which interfere with any consistent connection between
choice and successful productive achievement. However, if this
were all, one still might accept this in the social contract.
More to the heart of distributional fairness, there is a problem
that arises from the aim of society itself. All are to benefit
by means of the heterogeneous contributions of the persons who
are united in the society. All benefit from the heterogeneity
involved in the union. This cooperation (even with the diverse
private goals) itself is a public good. And the societal structure which grounds and supports the business institution depends
on such heterogeneous contributions. I am not sure if this maxim
to evaluate the practice of business would not hierarchize in
the "to each" of the practice an element so dependent on public
cooperation that, in the societal grounding of the practice itself, the basic element comes from each of the contributors
equally. So to hierarchize the distributed shares by the maxim
would be to have the maxim contradict itself.

By now we can see that even by modest survey there are problems with each of these suggestions for maxims of distributive
justice. There does not seem to be a single distributional maxim for economic benefits and burdens that does not need some
counterweight. Yet this survey has alerted us to what we would
want to mind, and what we would want to avoid. We are warned
against any maxim that would look to a static end-result only.
Rather we want a maxim in which a process is indicated, in which
there is a connection between contribution in the social dynamics wherein we share the burdens of production, and reception in
the social results wherein we share the benefits. We want freedom in the contribution, in order to respect each person's dignity, and we want a "floor" in the shares of benefits, in order
to respect each person's dignity. As much as possible, we want
to avoid any appeal to the perspective judgments of individuals
or government, yet we want some stability and supplementary adjustments when the process alone of a practice does not adequately handle human dignity, either in freedom of contribution (a
"fair" opportunity) or in a "floor" share of benefits.

There seems no perfect maxim available. Apparently all we
can have as a workable guide is one of several suboptimal alter-

natives. If this is true, then rational persons could agree correspondingly to a society that includes practices that function in a "not perfect, but better than others" manner. With this in mind, I offer the following maxim:

> "To each according to general contribution and according to the rules of the practice, with a 'floor' in respect to what economic benefits are needed effectively to exercise basic dignity and societal presence; and from each according to a fair opportunity choice and according to the rules of the practice."

This maxim could rationally be part of the social contract insofar as it has less shortcomings in its guidance of distribution than those maxims studied above. Consequently, in reference to distributive justice, insofar as the business institution as it exists in today's mixed economic system conforms to, or at least does not combat, this maxim, such a business institution is in principle ethically justified, and justicized.[7]

As a justicized subsystem in society, the institution of business can have those rules and practices, such as private management of the means of production, pricing according to a market, a standard of economic efficiency, etc., which are judged proper according to its special secondary horizon. These practices can be devised and followed ethically as long as the free and thoughtful self-ordering persons who compose the whole society could, in a situation of fairness, continue to agree to the institution.

Therefore, (1) the activities in the business institution can be ethically just insofar as they follow the practices that hold by consensus in business; and (2) the activities in the business institution can be ethically just insofar as the dynamic consensus of the people in society continue to accept, or to modify through government or social acts, the procedures that hold by consensus in business.

These conclusions carry an important suggestion for a resolution of the problem of the everyday dynamics of distributive justice. Given that the institution of business adequately satisfies the suboptimal maxim, then we can say, apriori, that the institution itself and those who operate under the secondary horizon of business are, insofar forth, "just" with respect to the ethics of distributive justice.

CHAPTER FIVE

ETHICS AND COMPETITION

"To Compete" : "To strive after in company with" (obsolete)

"Competition" : "The action of endeavoring to gain what another
                 at the same time endeavors to gain"; "a match
                 to determine relative excellence." (OED)

One has difficulty gaining a purchase on business competition because one not only faces a variety of phenomena under its rubric, but one also faces a variety of forms of competition in areas other than business, and one has a variety of customary opinion and psychological evidence about competition and its consequences. (It may be, however, that all instances of competition bear a "family resemblance" and that use in analysis of items such as game theory may not be out of place.) With appropriate caution, we may launch into this subject as one of the important "practices" of the business institution.

In competition, one seeks to maximize one's utilities (the amount of felt satisfaction one receives from any x) at the expense of others. This attitude is an assumption made in many economic studies about the typical "economic person." This model person is competitive in the sense that one is willing to achieve one's utility with the "double effect" of another's disutility. (See Chapter Three, III, C, for three possible variants of this self-interested economic person.) The person engages in those activities one has to do to secure part of a value for oneself in a situation in which others also are active with similar goals for themselves.

In this description, there arises a special factor that becomes important for the ethical analysis: the agent factor. This agent factor may be called the "fourth factor of production," in addition to land, labor, and capital. For our purposes, we identify the agent as the salaried manager. Put briefly, the manager tries, by organization, to maximize the economic utilities of a firm in the context of task fulfillment in a society. The manager does this in the arena of business with managers of other firms. This is the arena of competition in business.

One may match one's wits against a machine, natural forces, or the luck of the draw (which matching of wits is called a "one person game" or a "game against nature"), but such is significantly different from both the experience and the goal in business competition. In this arena, persons compete. And the arena is called the market.

41

The market is not a place. It is a term to indicate something very hard to handle conceptually. It indicates one of the three models of social and economic relationships.[1] For ethics, one must know the structures, contributions, and limits of each of these models.

(1)Exchange relationship (market). This model exhibits trade wherein both parties are considered to strive, by trade, toward higher utility functions. Here one says, "I do this if, or because, you do that."

(2)Command relationship (political). This model exhibits the authority of one party over another based on legal, moral, or physical superiority. Both parties may benefit in utilities by the relationship, but the relationship may be for the sake simply of the one or of the other, albeit the short-run utility of the command relation usually differs from its long-run utility. Here one says, "Do this or else I'll do that."

(3)Altruistic, Integrative, or Love relationship (friend). This model exhibits a community wherein one party so identifies with the other that the utility of the one is experienced in the utility of the other. Here one says, "I am better off when and only when you are better off." One should not consider this in too limited a way, for this is the model to explain one's share in the large area of "public goods" which are crucial for the union of persons in a society.

Some would justicize business competition solely within the model of exchange relationships. The approach usually takes classical or "pure" competition as an ideal, and interprets all deviations from classical competition in business as the fault of undesirable encroachment from command relationships in society.

I. Classical or "Pure" Competition

In a small firm engaged in "atomistic" competition, the manager does three things: buys factors in the factor market, combines them in the organized enterprise, and sells them in the market of goods and services. By "atomistic" I mean that each firm engaged in competition relevant to the manager's decisions is so small that any of the actions organized by the manager in any of the three areas of buying factors, combining factors, and selling goods and services, has no effect on either the market for factors or the market for goods and services. It is important to note that in atomistic competition, no individual manager has any market power.

Let me be precise on the claim that the manager of the atomistically competitive firm has no power on the market. Provided the firm can supply its product at the going price, the demand for its product is a horizontal line on a graph. In other words, the output of any one firm is too small to affect the equilibrium price for the market as a whole.

Yet the firm cannot expand its sales very much. Again a graph would show a cost curve where, as factor productivity declines, marginal costs soon rise above selling price.

Consequently, the manager operates within the limits of two horizontal curves: the market price for goods and the market price for factors. One faces a perfectly elastic supply of factors, meaning that one can hire all the factors marginal costs allow without changing prices at all in the factor market. Also one faces a perfectly elastic price curve, meaning that one can sell as much as one can produce without changing prices in the goods market either.[2]

Thus the manager of the atomistically competitive firm must organize all factors in the right proportions to have output as cheaply as possible against the set price to bring back maximum marginal revenue product. In other words, the manager will compare the returns to be had from all factors yielding the highest net return per dollar of cost, and will buy the most profitable input. Such decisions are within the power of the manager here.

It is to this model of atomistic competition that many economists refer by the phrase "pure competition." For there to be pure competition, several attributes of the market situation must obtain:

(1) a large number of firms in the position of sellers;
(2) a large number of individuals or firms in the position of buyers; (the minimum number to satisfy "large" here would be whatever number it would take in respect to a given commodity to insure that the individual seller or the individual buyer had the prices of factors and the prices of output forming those elastic horizontal curves which reflect a constancy in price throughout the schedule of factors and goods/services of which the firm is capable)
(3) easy entrance or exit as a seller or a buyer; (only with this attribute would the supply and demand schedules so shape a curve as to bring about the needed adjustments for equilibrium of price)
(4) the product has nothing distinctive, that is, the products of the many competitors are undifferentiated in quality; (only identical commodities really compete solely in respect to price. This means that the benchmark of atomistic competition is:)
(5) competition is in terms of price and of price alone;
(6) there must be adequate knowledge throughout the

participators in the market.

> (without adequate information, selling and buying would
> take place by those unable freely to enter or to leave
> the market, and selling and buying would take place in
> terms other than that of price alone. It is also impor-
> tant to note that the broadcast of such necessary infor-
> mation cannot adequately be provided by private firms.)

With little dispute, most experts agree on the above attributes of the market situation for pure competition. Most also
agree that, with the possible exception of a few kinds of small
businesses, pure competition is a model with no instances in the
real world. Strangely, many still go to the model to help explain business ethics. We now look at problems with such essays.

Many argue for the ethicality of atomistic competition in
business by reference to the "function" of the competition. The
argument starts as follows.

> Business competition is the mechanism that makes the best
> possible use of economic factors so that these function to
> coordinate human efforts. (A Utilitarian framework)
> Where it exists, competition guides individual efforts bet-
> ter than any other mechanism available. It is the norm for
> those actions by which certain elements of economic signif-
> icance expand or contract, by which certain goods and ser-
> vices are selected as best in society, whereby efficiency
> in production and distribution is rewarded, and whereby
> goods and services are reasonably priced and distributed.

The words "best" and "better" are valuations so far left ambiguous. One may ask, by reference to which horizon does one understand "best" and "better" here? Competition will be judged good
derivatively once we identify such an horizon, because competition's values as a mechanism are derivative values.

Usually those who use this argument appeal with these value
terms both to the economic and to the liberty horizons, both to
"best in reference to economic efficiency" and to "best in reference to individual freedom." By the economic horizon, one evaluates on grounds of efficiency, flexible prices for the sake of
free allocation, and the advantage in distribution of income on
the side of the buyer or consumer. By the liberty horizon, one
evaluates on the grounds that we carry on economic activities in
a social setting "without coercive or arbitrary intervention of
political authority."[3] Thus, the defenders of the atomistically
competitive market refer to both these horizons and claim such
a market serves both society and business.

Such justification looks to the procedure by which a society
distributes material resources effectively for the society and

it looks to the medium in which free buyers and sellers can enter and leave the economic market. From this justification, one could explain such terms as "unfair" or "unethical" competition, in that such terms indicated the violation of one of the six attributes of the classical model of competition. One could also discern instances where one would classify a business phenomenon "unfair" but add that it was unfair not because of a violation of the practice of competition. Rather the phenomenon could be unethical in ways not specific to competitive practice, such as unfairness in the original situation, or in ways accidentally combined with competitive practice but not essential to it, such as misleading claims in advertising, or shortweighing in deliveries.

But is one who acts competitively assuredly ethical, or must competition have boundaries for its attitude and activities to be ethical? Do we have principles to support the position that there must be limits to what one individual is willing to do to gain utilities at the expense of others, what one is willing to do to take business away from others?

To guage answers one must ponder the distinction between the pure process justice of a practice and the fairness of the practice itself. It is one thing to say that an activity or attitude ethically is just according to a given practice, and quite another to say that the practice itself is fair. The practice itself must be judged by some higher horizon. But an activity according to the rules of an operative societal practice would be in itself ethically just according to the horizon of the practice. Thus, in matters of atomistically pure competition, with its two points for justification mentioned above, one could claim that attitudes and actions within such competition are ethical because they are instances of the practice. They are justicized in a "purely procedural way," no matter the starting point or the outcome.

F. A. Hayek seems to claim this and he denies that pure competition is to be judged by any reference to an end-dependent egalitarian distribution of outcome.[4] Hayek first argues that one cannot criticize the outcome of business activities by the standard of proportionality of reward to moral merit. He argues with Hume that such proportionality, given the limits on human knowledge, is not practicable. And he argues that it is not desirable to have any practice wherein one's position in society depends finally upon human ideas of moral merit. Such, he says, would essentially vitiate a free society.

This first defense has two major weaknesses. First, it ignores the distinction between that which may be due a person because of effort (merit right), and that which may be due a person because one is a human being in a society (dignity right).

One cannot assume apriori that all economic distributions are
neutral. Even if a society wishes to be "free" and not distribute material portions on someone's idea of moral merit, still
that same society may wish to be "free" and make sure there is
distribution of material portions according to some ideal of
human dignity (i.e., at least a "floor" distribution).

Second, the defense ignores those dissatisfactions one experiences with the insistence that the outcomes of free market
interplay, conceived as the results of impersonal accidents, be
the major factors that determine claims in a society to those
goods which most correlate with property, power, and prestige.
Is there something lacking in competition that is blind?

Hayek calls for a justicization of blind competition analogous to the justicization of blind application of law in the ju-
ridical practice.[5] He adroitly offers the analogy with the emphasis on the blindness of application with no respect for persons. Unfortunately, the cause of the "no respect" in law is to
insure that the laws apply universally. For business competition, the "no respect" refers to the chance and good luck that
are "often as important as skill and foresight in determining
the fate of different people." Yet we would certainly object
when chance and good luck are the operative elements in the
blindness of legal justice.

The argument must be framed more effectively. So Hayek
drops the "blind" analogy and sets up an either-or.

> "The choice open to us is not between a system in which
> everybody will get what he deserves according to some abso-
> lute and universal standard of right, and one where the in-
> dividual shares are determined partly by accident or good
> or ill chance, but between a system where it is the will of
> a few persons that decides who is to get what, and one
> where it depends at least partly on the ability and enter-
> prise of the people concerned and partly on unforeseeable
> circumstances."[6]

The argument by Hayek on the justice of competition comes down
to the utilitarian "it may not be perfect, but it is far more
congruent with human freedom and thus with human dignity than
any alternative possible." He presents as the primary alternative a situation wherein a few persons, on apparently idiosyncratic whim, make up some rules for distribution of economic outputs which rules cannot intelligibly be defended without the
idiosyncratic principle.

Ultimately Hayek's case for the justicization of atomistic
competition is that only this procedure acknowledges that business must be judged primarily as a process, and not by its out-

come. Any judgment on its outcome would depend upon idiosyncratic rules made up by a few persons. Thus Hayek forms an argument not only for the irrelevancy of justice to the outcome of
business competition, but also for the decisiveness of the process itself for the question of justice, and he bases both on
the principle of liberty.

One might be drawn to agree except, so far, one aspect has
not been probed: the starting point for any and all exchange relationships of the market. One could argue that the process
alone decides justice, but only as long as it is fair on all
sides. The procedures with its rules which determine who succeeds and who fails will be fair and acceptable only with reference to the broader fairness of the societal situation.[7]

To say that competition is a justicized procedure only when
it is fair says more than first appears. It says that American
society really is ambivalent with respect to business competition. We do not accept the description of business competition
as "anarchy with a policeman." We want certain qualities in the
institutional structures within which competition occurs. And
we do not think that justice is served unless there is common
acknowledgment of these structures.

It is this commonality, this shared sense of what is required that holds important implications for justice in business
competition. To share a sense of what is required implies that
we share a social milieu for the competition. We are together
in many ways and share many goals and values that are to be expressed in and by our procedures. We could not reach and enjoy
these goals and values in isolation, and it is false to describe
pertinent experiences as ones of simple and pure mutual instru-
mentality of private individuals.

The call for fairness in the situation and the procedures
that are competitive, therefore, implies that the liberty that
is valuable in such is not any "anarchy with a policeman," wherein everyone tries to get away with whatever one can without getting caught. Such a liberty is not a real value in competition
because it is not the value of liberty in society itself. We
frown on "any means to winning" because this attitude ignores
that there is a more basic relationship level in society besides
the exchange relationship between isolated individuals who act
only by competitive calculations with each other.[8]

Thus for the competition to be fair, the starting point as
well as the procedures must be acceptable. And since every outcome is itself contributory to a subsequent starting point, I am
not yet convinced that some adjustments are not required before
a purely procedural justicization of atomistic competition in
business can be effected.

Ideally, the analysis of pure competition in business has as given all competitors on an equal footing, all powerlessly facing the two horizontal curves of the price of factors and the price of demanded quantity by buyers. As such, one might say that the initial situation was fair, that is, that situation which would be agreed to by thoughtful and free persons who wished to enter the arena and all of whom had freely to agree on the setup beforehand. As we know, today's world of business has elements in it other than this ideal setup. So one is not overly troubled with the incompleteness of the justicization of the practice of pure competition, since the resolution of any problems remaining therein is moot.

II. Oligopolistic Competition

It is obvious that any atomistically competitive firms share all of today's business markets with other competitive phenomena. There still are many firms that face horizontally elastic price curves for factors and outputs, but these are lumped now in the general set of the "powerless majority" of our corporational society. More and more, attention has turned to those firms that have a relatively large share of the assets or of the output or of the sales in various "industries" of business markets. For example, if there are some sixty odd thousand firms in transportation, communication, and utilities, but if less than one hundred control nearly eighty percent of the assets in the field, we no longer speak of atomistically competitive firms. Likewise, if the top firm makes twenty-five percent, or if the top four firms make fifty percent of the commodity marketed, there is something other in the industry than atomistic competition. For many of the basic markets in business today, for example, steel, automobiles, beer, chemicals, drugs, electrical appliances, airlines, farm machinery, breakfast cereal, soap, tobacco, and so on, concentration ratios of oligopolistic measure are the rule rather than the exception. Heilbroner and Thurow distinguish the phenomenon as the difference between "price takers" and "price searchers."[9] "There are so few firms that each one faces a downward sloping demand curve. That means that each firm, by varying its output, can affect the price of its product," because it can significantly affect total supply.

For our purposes, the paramount change the phenomenon of an oligopolistic top to many basic markets introduces is: "power over the price of goods and services and even, in modern large corporations, over factors." Once the price is no longer is the free flow of the market, then the tendency of the market to find equilibrium which equalizes income so that there will not be long term profits in a given field is impaired. In all high concentration industries there is a significantly high profit rate in comparison with the pure competition model. The profitability also is a factor in entry-barriers. Moreover, with a lack of product differentiation, advertising enters with the high profit rate, and thus in turns acts as a further entry-barrier.

One recalls that part of the justification of a competitive business system rested on the freedom of entry and exit with respect to the market, which ultimately meant that the consumer was king, and on the service to the entire society in the expansion and contraction of demand which controls allocation of resources. With oligopolies, such justification is irrelevant.

What changes in justification can we find as we move from a model of atomistic competition to whatever model approximates our real world of business economy? Initially, there are some strong utilitarian arguments for oligopoly. (a)Pure competition seems incompatible with scale efficiency. In some industries, economies of scale dictate that production of goods or services be concentrated to facilitate achievement. (b)Pure competition seems incompatible with the research and development necessary for a dynamic growth dependent somewhat upon invention and innovation. Joseph Schumpeter argued that big firms were necessary for the kind of research and development in our economy.[10] (c)American competition has grown coupled with the conviction that it is advantageous that the people who are to be customers have income which can buy goods produced at maximum output with maximum distribution. Thus, it has been part of American competition that the number of hours of work required to earn money to buy a given item should steadily decline. Consequently, the oligopolistic situation has given the average American the highest standard of consumer goods living ever enjoyed by the majority of a country's population.[11]

For the ethician, neither size nor profits are the major concern, power is. Let us make sure there is some clarity in the phrase, "an oligopolistic firm has some power over the market. The firm that experiences a downward sloping demand curve has market power. It has the possibility of choice, decisions, and multiple goals in its operations. Alfred D. Chandler, Jr., writes: "In many sectors of the economy the visible hand of management replaced what Adam Smith referred to as the invisible hand of market forces. . . . (T)he salaried managers of a relatively small number of large mass producing, large mass retailing, and large mass transporting enterprises coordinated current flows of goods through the processes of production and distribution and allocated the resources to be used for future production and distribution in major sectors of the American economy.[12]

This market power means that the phenomenon of competition can no longer be separated from the decisions of the managers themselves. Moreover, since managers with market power could survive even if they add noneconomic elements to their decisions, the onus of explanation if they do not do so when it is socially important lies on their shoulders unaided by appeal to the demands of "pure competition." To deny the possibility of the presence of noneconomic elements in such decisions in any apriori manner sppears to be gratuitous.

Even more, when one considers that oligopolistic managers not only face a downward sloping demand curve, but also employ advertising and are benefitted by peer impelled consumerism in a society with a high standard of living, one must also note that the demand curve itself can be shifted to the right and that there is thereafter a strong tendency for the shifted demand curve to remain inelastic with respect to movement back to the left. This shift of the demand curve becomes, to some extent, a dependent variable for business decisions.[13]

Clare Griffin suggests that any company in business, no matter if it may be oligopolistic, still faces competition if the firm's managers find it necessary to adapt business decisions to meet the activities of rivals, present or potential, regardless whether these rivals are in the same "industry" or not. Mr. Griffin's suggestion implies that we should drop singular concentration on price when we speak of competition and focus on the extent to which business managers conduct their affairs with awareness of the actual or possible actions of others.[14]

Leon Hickman suggests that we should not think that what we want from competition is an efficient allocation of resources in the short run. Perhaps our utilitarian goal as a society is to improve such an allocation over a long period of time. Such long term allocation would support social acceptability for big scale economies even at the cost of less freedom for entering and leaving the buyer-seller market. Hickman goes on to list eight observations which would aid us to rethink the growth, intensity, and nature of the current corporational competition.[15]

(1) Dynamically improved communications and transportation systems and an increased population have fundamentally sharpened competition. (2) Increased competition has developed in the form of new business methods and new types of business organizations (such as supermarkets, discount stores, and auto rental companies). (3) New products, processes and services constantly intensify the competitiveness of the economy (because they provide substitutive competition and thus elasticity for buyers). (4) Changes in living patterns and a rising level of discretionary income are intensifying competition (such as increased leisure and the evolvement of many durables into necessities). (5) The expansion of technological research in recent years has intensified competition. The time between invention and production has been so reduced that even if now alone in a field, one always faces a threat. (6) The growth of large-scale enterprise has increased competition in a number of ways, for example, the

improved education and training techniques. (7)Expanding foreign competitors is a large factor today. (8)At the most, price
competition is but a small part of the story of today's competitive activities.

In an oligopolistic market situation, then, several aspects
have changed from the atomistically competitive market situation.
(a)The number of firms has been reduced. This may be in terms
of an absolute number, or in terms of a few firms who have the
majority of the assets, sales, or quantity supplied in the market. (b)Ease of entrance and exit by either supplier or buyer
has changed. (c)The change on the side of the seller is in
terms of economies of scale and managerial coordination of factors and allocation. (d)Emphasis on differentiation of product
has changed. The change has been most effected by technology
and advertising.

The oligopolistic firm still confronts a demand curve that,
as such, is out of its control. Yet it can try to do something
to affect the demand curve by advertising. It can try to move
the demand curve to the right, or try to change the slope of the
curve. In these efforts, the firm attempts to gain long-term
success. But advertising in turn means that the oligopolistic
firm must incur a selling cost that is not required of the atomistically competitive firm, as the advertising tries to distinguish the product or service as somehow differentiated.

This usually is the heart: product/service differentiation.
Even though it experiences power over price, factor coordination, and allocation, the oligopolistic firm usually finds price
competition too risky. As for prices, there usually is in the
oligopolistic concentration in an industry the appearance of
what is termed a "price leader." One firm (or a few firms) sets
a price and all else follow, even without overt collusion. Such
price leaders often "target" their prices in order to obtain a
certain yearly return, after taxes, on the yearly investment.
With this procedure profits are not competed away, and the consumer surplus that occurs in pure competition here is transferred
over to the sellers. Part of this strategy consists in the decision of the firms not to produce up to capacity. An auto firm,
for example, decides to produce "x" number of cars in its plants
and targets prices so as to make a profit even if only 60 percent
of the year's production is sold.

But the more important strategy involves the ability of the
firm's managers to find or to create people's demands.[16] Management planning, from being an automatic response to market
forces, contains here a decision element important not only for
business success within the business horizon, but also important
for business success within the societal horizon. With the fore-
going preliminaries, what of the ethics of this competition?

52

III.   Competition and Ethics

One of the first persons to examine the ethics of business competition, Frank H. Knight, suggested that the examination will fall naturally into three parts.[17]

(A) First, competition is supposed to be a mechanism for the production and distribution of goods and services that people want, that is, it is a means to an end stated in terms of want-satisfaction.   But which wants and whose wants are to be satisfied? "The system's answer to this two-fold question constitutes its social economic value scale."[18]

Besides this two-fold question, the first part of the examination has two more inquiries: the efficiency of the system in respect to the values it recognizes, and the provisional character of wants and the obvious fact that the wants which an economic system operates to gratify are largely produced by the workings of the system itself.

(B) The second part of the examination (fresh in Knight's writing, but more common today) turns on a recognition that the motive in business is to a significant extent "emulation as such."[19]   "Industry and trade is a competitive game, in which men engage in part from the same motives as in other games or sports."   Here we do not find simple economic want-satisfaction. The question for this second part will be: what kind of game is business, and what relation does the game of business have to ethics?   (We will find it useful to examine the game ethics of business in terms of a secondary horizon in ethics.)

(C) The third part of the examination looks to the relation of business values and business ethics to fundamental values and fundamental ethics.   (We have termed this the relation of a secondary horizon in ethics to a fundamental horizon in ethics.) Competition in the economic order has supported and furthered making emulation and rivalry an essential cultural characteristic of our society.   "The modern idea of enjoyment as well as of achievement has come to consist chiefly in keeping up with or getting ahead of other people in a rivalry for things about whose significance, beyond furnishing objectives for the competition, little question is asked."[20]

According to Knight, these three parts of the inquiry into the ethics of competition in business must be done together, for economic activity is simultaneously in all three dimensions of human activities: the formation and satisfaction of wants; game competition; and the models of self-expression in society.   We will have to keep this interconnectedness in mind as we artificially divide the three and look at them in order.

IV. (A) Values and Efficiency

For the first part of the examination, the relevant questions are: what value demands are created and satisfied (or not);
whose demands are created and satisfied (or not); the efficiency
of the system in regards to these values; and the self-perpet-
uating production of demands by the system.

1. _What values_. Price alone translates demands for the
atomistic competition situation. Those who cannot pay, cannot
enter the market. Consequently, the movements of demand and the
wants satisfied with price as an independent variable cannot be
regarded as indicative of anything other than a value within the
horizon of the system itself. Hence such cannot be subsequently
used to justicize the competition system itself. One begs the
ethical question here to set atomistic competition as a reliable
guide to what ought to be values for persons. To attempt this
would be to move invalidly from description (what is) to norm
(what ought to be).

Unless the economic market were the only locus for values
and unless all persons found their values therein, one could not
apriori equate "will and ability to buy and sell" goods and services with the human values relevant to the judgment on business
competition. But the business market is not the only locus (for
we still seek values when economic wants are satisfied) and not
all of us with economic wants find satisfaction through the market (we cannot all enter the market).

The situation is significantly altered in today's business
world, but the alteration exaggerates the limited value schedule
in the business horizon and does not ameliorate the limitation.
The corporate manager's search for scale sales or large margins
per unit sales coupled with low risk may cause economic tension,
but such often curtails quality and variety even within the business goods and services themselves. We will comment on quality
variance a little later.

2. _Whose values_. Since we cannot all enter the market for
all the goods there, and since we do not find all our values in
the market, one can deduce there is a spectrum among people according to how each one's values are more down through less satisfied through the market. Still with reference to atomistic
market situations, we can state simply that those who can enter
the market and who have values which are original or are created
by the economic system are those who have relatively high satisfaction by the system.

With the oligopolistic situation there are new values, but
we must modify our statement only slightly. Of the new values
---lessening of business risk; comfortableness of managers in

salaries, benefits, and perquisites; reluctance to break from
safe but technologically inefficient processes; stress on sales-
manship---many are on the side of the business firms. However,
it would be demagogic to weigh only the producer's voice in the
origination of the new wants on the side of the consumer. The
answer to "whose values" always is "those who can enter and gain
any power in the market." And the discretionary income of consumers has risen significantly in the last thirty years.

However, we must also acknowledge that the price mechanism
alone, as Knight saw, is unreliable as a measure of people's
values. The individuals who buy are not as equal in fact as
they are in theory in estimating the quality of the goods and
services available. Due to the advantage differentials from
social condition, age, and the like, individuals use discretionary income irrationally at times.

And an appeal to utility fares little better, due especially
to our growing alertness to the effects of envy, impulse, and ig-
norance. The wants of people are at least as "other-directed"
today as before and this raises as yet unanswered questions on
the adequacy in resource allocation when done according to any
expression of such wants.

3. Efficiency. Just how efficient is the market even in
respect to its own economic values? Two aspects will be looked
at here: the reward schedule for participants, and the strategy
of underengineering and waste.

On the side of the producer, the distribution of any competitive system has a reward schedule for the participants. Knight
thinks there should be the distribution of claims on the reward
schedule for participants according to talent, effort, and luck.
According to our "natural moral sentiment," perhaps the greatest
of these should be effort. However, with only "dollar votes" to
set the reward schedule itself, the relative pricing of items
within the system, wherein untalented or non-effort items meet
the tastes and the purchasing power of buyers, the efficiency of
distribution is shortcircuited. Who gains reward and how much
is gained are not according to human need or human effort. The
value question of such a means to distribute producer rewards
remains unsettled.

Knight admits that there also is a question whether the
principle of distribution according to effort, even if it were
achieved, could be reconciled with the principle of distribution
according to efficiency, or the principle of fairness in the
"game" competition.[21] For efficiency one would give more tools
to those who best could use them. For effort one would reward
variously according to a schedule of more or less effort. For
fairness one would want all to start with equal opportunity to

compete well. These three ideals cannot help but be in conflict, which means that efficiency is weakened with any move in the direction of the other two.

One of the trickiest decisions for a manager comes with the discovery that underengineering, or controlled obsolescence, increases the market activity and thereby functions in long-term planning. Usually, also, while decreasing the cost of individual products and lowering the initial market price, underengineering still permits a higher profit per unit cost. There are several kinds of underengineering for the sake of controlled obsolescence, among which are the following.

a) The use of frequent (e.g., yearly) superficial changes, say, in styling.
b) The acceptance of broader tolerance limits in quality during the manufacturing process for the sake of mass production.
c) The deliberate underengineering so that products wear out more rapidly than they could be manufactured to do.
d) The deliberate holding back of product improvements until sales for existing models drop or until a competitor issues the improved product.
e) The production of psychological dissatisfaction in the mind of the consumer with an adequate old product.

Some obvious examples of underengineered goods in these five are many lines of clothing, toys, razor blades, light bulbs, car batteries, most American automobiles, and air conditioners.

Each of these kinds of underengineering deserves a separate comment.

a) The frequent change kind of underengineering need not always be evaluated unfavorably. Ordinarily, the consumer is not buying just the superficial changes in style or prestige appeal, but also several hidden improvements. The superficial changes often are merely attention-getters and even they can be a value if limited to this role.

b) The acceptance of broader tolerance limits is an acceptable deficiency for the sake of mass production if the entire procedure is for widespread distribution and reasonable profits. However, producing a poor product with the intention of keeping repairmen happy when the product is installed is not acceptable even on the economic efficiency level.

c) Deliberate underengineering for shorter product life must be justified by a greater good than any sacrificed, especially when the practice threatens the atmosphere of trust wherein the consumer expects a decent product and the assumed contract on the side of the producer to give out a professionally made prod-

uct. Underengineering must either encourage innovation or it
must contribute to the quality of later products. But in both
of these possibilities, there is also the question of present
need and present waste. How much unnecessary waste goes on, and
how many real needs are not being met through unnecessarily
rapid wearing-out are questions constantly challenging this
practice. And how many contracting consumers are left to walk
in misunderstanding of what they are buying cannot ethically be
ignored.

d)The holding back of new models may be requisite business
practice for the sake of inventory balance. It does not seem to
be unethical as long as earlier models are adequate and no falsification concerning future plans takes place.

e)The production of psychological obsolescence involves
persuading the consumer to buy new goods and services before the
presently held item has exhausted its usefulness. The evaluation of this practice necessitates a look at the production of
demands by the system.

4. _Production of demands_. The inquiry into the ethics of
the production of demands by the economic system has many levels.
Some of these we leave to the chapter on Advertising. Here we
will be brief and general.

The first distinction of importance separates those demands
that arise from new availability thanks to the innovations and
the rising discretionary income, those demands that enter expectations thanks to the satisfaction of more original and subsis-
tential wants, and those demands that come as a result of the
mechanism of the business system, either by accident or by design. The ethical approach to the first two differs from that
for the third because the former two concern an outcome of the
business system, the latter concerns procedures within it.

For brevity's sake here, I comment only on the third set of
demands. I confine these comments to deliberate procedures within the system meant and intended to produce demands in consumers.
Many have criticized such production as inefficient, a wasteful
compounding of the problem of allocation of resources. These
persons point out that advertising (the most common procedure
employed) costs, and that such costs mean that the consumer pays
a price that is more than the lowest cost necessary to ensure
the availability of the product.[22] But the more telling ethical
attack on advertising as wasteful aims at the effort to form or
to change consumers' tastes. The formation or change of these
demands is a function of psychological, not physical, needs and
a function of a declining marginal utility of income.[23]

Such an attack has some important presuppositions. (a)Ad-

vertising that is not "constructive"(i.e., that does not give
the consumer information or some other useful service) gives no
significant service to the consumer. (b)Advertising that is not
"constructive" disregards the original needs and demands of
consumers.

We will study these more in the chapter on Advertising.
But for now I might say two things. First, F. A. Hayek has noted
with some accuracy that there is no reason to assume apriori that
all human wants of significance must be clearly formed prior to
the activities of others in the society.[24] I might add that it
is either by peer example or by other social publicity, such as
advertising, that real and important human wants are specified.
Without such examples or publicity, the original needs and demands may remain frustratingly unspecific. In other words, one
need not accept without qualification the presuppositions against
advertising that is not "constructive." Thus, apriori, there is
nothing determinate ethically concerning advertising with respect
to efficiency or demand production. In both areas, how advertising is used in specific matters must be judged.

Second, the interrelationship of consumption and expanded
production has been an essential factor in the rising standard
of living in society. And this would base a prima facie utilitarian justification for encouraging consumption.

V. (B) Competition and Games

Ludwig Wittgenstein has warned us that, at best, games have
but a family resemblance to each other. So we hesitate to give
a general definition that will be adequate to all those endeavors we term "games." Yet enough has been written about game theory pertinent to our discussion that we can engage in some gen-
eralized reflection to assist our grasp of an ethics of competition. We are helped by game theory to see a little better
exactly what is the rationality of a good game player within the
horizon of game competition.

Knight mentions as qualities relative to the interest one
has in any game the three elements of ability, effort, and
luck.[25] Ability to play is a combination, like all human capabilities, of innate endowment and education acquired from previous expenditure of effort in play or in practice or in some
comparable activity. Effort comes as the game compels the players to exert full energy and ability. Luck comes as the element
that meets the demand that the outcome be unpredictable. The
balance between these three will control the interest of the
players.

Normally in game theory one does not spend too much time

on games whose outcome depends solely on the decision of individual players plus "mere luck." In such games as solitaire, roulette, faro, craps, one does analysis by a look at probability tables. Such games are called "one person games," or "games against nature." There are various categories of such games, and the distinctions depend upon the function of "nature" in the game.

It is more to our purpose to look at games wherein one uses the element of strategy and also rationality to think out the strategy. These portions of game theory have been found of some application to decisions in economics, business, and politics. The foundations of game theory so applicable were laid by John von Neumann who, in 1928, wrote a paper on strategy in poker which included exposition of the important "minimax" theorem, and who, with Oskar Morgenstern, in 1944, published Theory of Games and Economic Behavior.

Before we reflect on the ethics involved, let me summarize briefly the essence of game theory in business and list some common terminology. In essence, game theory in business functions in decisions among alternatives wherein the decisions of others will affect which is the best decision for oneself. We assume that there are two or more loci of decisions and each decision unit acts rationally, which in this horizon means "with a view toward self-gain." Game theory concerns choice problems in situations of conflicts of interests. The best choice for anyone depends on what one expects the other(s) to do, and one realizes that the other is guided by reciprocal expectations. Thus, there is interdependence in the game. Game theory tries to remove the uncertainty by idealizing assumptions about rationality and about the universality of self-interest of all players.

A choice must be made from several alternatives (A_1, A_2,... A_n) and the relative desirability of each depends on which choice is made by the other player (B_1, B_2,...B_n). To each pair (A_i, B_j), there will be a consequence outcome (the set of which are summarized on a payoff matrix by means of a utility function, cardinal or ordinal). With respect to any decision problem, the set of alternatives is assumed to form a mutually exclusive and exhaustive listing of those alternatives that are relevant to the decision and about which there is uncertainty.

Terminological Definitions in the analysis of game strategy:

a) outcome of game: the physical issue from the physical activities of the players;
b) payoff of game: the value to the players of the outcome;
c) finite: there are a certain number of alternatives per player, and the game ends after a certain number of moves;

d) perfect information: there are no surprises; all that went
    before and all future possibilities are part of each play-
    er's own decision process (e.g., chess, GO, checkers);
e) general: somehow, the information a player has for use in
    decisions is imperfect (normal business situation);
f) zero-sum game: game of pure conflict; the interests of the
    players are so diametrically opposed that the sum of win-
    ning-losing is always zero, for the value involved is sta-
    tic and wealth is neither created nor destroyed in the game;
    every gain for one is an equivalent loss for another;
g) non zero-sum game: game in any way different from zero-sum:
    there is mutual dependence as part of logical structure of
    game and all hope to gain somewhat since wealth is created
    in the game process;
h) solution: that which the players can do within the rules of
    the game. There are two general categories of solutions:
    cooperative and non-cooperative;
i) non-cooperative solution: one player tries to act in such an
    independent way so as to achieve the best possible results
    no matter what others do (e.g., poker, pure competition);
j) cooperative solution: the individual player looks to what one
    can gain by coordination with others over and above the
    value one could gain by going it alone (e.g., team sports,
    unions, oligopolistic price targeting);
k) strategy: one's plan for decisions in non-cooperative solu-
    tion;
l) coalition: one's plan for decisions in cooperative solution;
m) rational: the player always seeks more of some utility. In
    games there can be three levels of rationality: individual,
    group, and societal;
n) individual rationality: the player seeks more no matter what
    others do;
o) group rationality: one seeks as member of a group more than
    what one could get individually;
p) societal rationality: one seeks as member of society more than
    what one could get as individual or as group member.

    Since game theory started in an examination of poker, let
us look briefly at this game. The heart of poker which allows
for strategy is the making of bids by the players (let us call
them A and B). After a bid is made by player A, player B has
the option of folding, seeing, or raising. Even though as player B makes a decision, player B knows the action of player A,
there is still an element in poker that makes the game a general
game (of imperfect information). This is the element of "bluffing."[26]

    To start with, if player A has a strong hand, player A has
reason to expect to win and so would make high bets and numerous
raises. Consequently, player B may assume if player A makes

high bets and raises that player A has a strong hand. Player B
with a moderate hand has a reason for a decision to fold. However, if B folds, the hands are not compared. Thus player A may
have taken an advantage of this rule and, even with a weak hand,
have given the false impression of strength by a high bid or
raise, hoping to get player B to fold.

Actual bluffing, of course, is not that simple. If player
A is known to big high only on strong hands, his opponent will
likely always fold. And so player A will not be able to gain
much by strong hands. Yet if player A bluffs constantly, player B, knowing this, will call the bluffs and gain in the long
run. Thus, the aim of player A is to create uncertainty in the
mind of player B as to the correlation between A's bets and the
strength of A's hands. The two real motives behind the bluffing,
consequently, are the desire to give a false impression of
strength in real weakness and the desire to give a false impression of weakness in real strength. "Both are instances of inverted signaling. . .i.e., of misleading the opponent."

"Bluffing," therefore, is a means to control the kind of
information one's opponent may have to use in a decision, and an
effort to mislead the opponent as to the real situation through
such controlling. This appears to be a neat example of a secondary horizon. In the game, one can legitimately expect that
the opponent is able to interpret the bidding that is the bluff
or that might be a bluff. For the reference horizon is one of
strategy. Therefore, at least within the situation of the game,
all else being equal, the use of the bluff is ethically good.

VI. Business Competition as Zero-Sum
Non-Cooperative Poker

There is no doubt that in the field of corporational business there are certain rules that govern the acceptable interplay
of top managers and middle managers both within a company and
between companies. Albert Z. Carr has trenchantly described this
atmosphere as analogous to a poker-game, wherein the rules are
the state and the federal laws, and the strategies within these
laws are as cutthroat as in poker, with but a few practices,
such as playing in cahoots or holding back chips owed the pot,
still considered unsportsmanlike. The central question Mr. Carr
asks is "Is Business Bluffing Ethical?"[27] Against the charge
that he presumes the answer to be yes, Mr. Carr responds:[28]

This complaint seems to me extraordinary. More than once,
the article stresses the values of truth-telling and integrity in business, where, certainly, there are as many high-
minded men as one will find in most walks of life. My point
is that, given the prevailing ethical standards of business,
an executive who accepts those standards and operates

accordingly is guilty of nothing worse than conformity; he is merely playing the game according to the rules and the customs of society.

And Mr. Carr comments on the strength and weaknesses of the analogy of business strategy to poker:[29]

> Like all useful analogies, this one was intended to throw light on the subject, not to provide an exact parallel. The honorable poker player who, within the laws of the game, takes pleasure in outsmarting the other fellow has many a counterpart in the paneled offices of the corporate hier-archies. Again, it may be noted that there is no compulsion for any executive to mislead others, any more than there is for the poker player to bluff. The option is his; most players exercise it at one time or another.

One may note here the three parallels between poker and this business strategy: in the option to enter the game, in the de-mand to interpret, and in the resultant uncertainty in the mind of the opponent. Within the horizon of the poker game there can-not exist any credibility that should be given to the overt statements or moves by an opponent. Even if the opponent asserts there is no bluff, how is one ever sure that the assertion itself is not the bluff? All decisions herein are decisions of strate-gy. The horizon for interpretation is success in competition using all advantages and being limited only by actual rules. The rules of poker are not the rules of everyday behavior.

Poker is a non-cooperative zero-sum game. In poker, the heart of strategy is the making of bids which, as we have seen, implies inverted signalling intended to create uncertainty in and mislead opponents. Hence in poker one correctly distrusts others, ignores claims of friendship, and knows that cunning, deception, and concrealment of strength, weaknesses, and in-tentions are vital.[30]

The ethics of poker cannot be judged by everyday private person ethical standards. Yet "no one thinks any the worse of poker on that account." Lived attitudes in business show enough similarities so that, by a mode of analogy, some would verify that the ethics of business likewise cannot be judged by every-day private person ethical standards. The argument by analogy, of course, does not demand complete parallels. All decisions may be decisions of strategy, but not all decisions need be in terms of a non-cooperative zero-sum game. In business, one could have game rationality as one of a group, or even as one of a society, and a cooperative solution, as defined, means that the individual player can gain by cooperation over and above any value one could gain by going it alone.

The thrust of the analogy is the imputed acceptance in the game of business of practices that would not be acceptable in the actions of those in business when those persons act outside the business horizon. At times "to tell the truth but not the whole truth in public disclosure," "to hold back the better product for a time,""to exaggerate,""to seek to reduce hostility in government or in the public at large"---all these are decisions of strategy. If one is "ethical," it is because "it pays to be ethical," or because "good ethics is good business." If it did not pay, or if it were not good business, at least one would have to rethink one's strategy.

If it is a fact that such practices within the business institution are known and at least are not openly condemned, the ethician insists that this fact still does not validate an "ought to be." We can still ask,"ought such poker-like strategies to be the case in business?" To begin an answer, I would here abstract from the individual and societal rights affected and evaluate business bluffing directly and in itself by a utilitarian mode of verification. There seem to be two dangers endemic within any poker-strategy ethics.

(1) Such encouragement of aggression against others, since it would apply most of one's time of active decision making, probably desensitizes ethical responding to others, at least in those areas where the aggression occurs. As in the game of war, competition strategy has the sequential result of partial raising of ethical thresholds.

(2) Such encouragement probably contributes to a decay of the fiducial framework within other social levels. Ironically this would be a tendency more in times when the public demands that business be "honest like an ordinary person" than in earlier times when business did not have to "answer to Congress." In earlier times, one was more sure how to interpret the actions of those in business, and so the danger to the atmosphere of trust in society was not as great.

Before further comments on the ethics of game competition, one should look at a few differences in coalition games.

VII. Business Coalition Games

The game of oligopolistic competition has specific albeit unwritten rules. The goal of the game is growth for all the members of the industry, and radical price or radical technology challenges generally are out of bounds. Fair competitive tactics include advertising, customer service, product design, cost-cutting and product differentiation. This last itself is a strategy for cost-cutting, for it aims to increase one's share

of the market at minimum cost. (One should include here a note
on the local retailer who emphasizes product differentiation by
means of brand-name identity or the retailer's service identity.
For such, there may be a slight downward slope experienced in
the demand curve and thus a slight modification in the direction
of the oligopolistic game. However, the world of local sales,
in which all have about the same products, also has many elements
of pure competition.)

In an oligopolistic game, since there are parallel as well
as opposed interests (non zero-sum), the players may engage in
a cooperative solution with group rationality. (This does not
necessarily involve collusion.) In the oligopolistic situation,
the game has a "core" of large sellers who operate with group
rationality, usually with the assistance of a "price leader."
(At the "fringe" the game has a set of smaller sellers who compete in the industry by a non-cooperative solution with individual rationality which includes a "non-disturbance" rule in
reference to the large sellers.) The "core" is thus a kind of
optimality solution that resists change.[31] There is a "core"
because the game has payoffs and a way to distribute payoffs so
that no member of the coalition can do better by withdrawing.
Each player is rational for each is better off in this particular coalition than in any other possible position. Obviously,
coalitions have the property of supporting stability, even without collusion. And since controlling values for large businesses
include this stability, the lessening of risk, and the increase
of receipts, a core solution is quite attractive.

There is, nevertheless, always restlessness in a coalition.
For it obtains if and only if the managers find it rational. So
in one sense, as long as there are several managers, one will
always find competition. For the several managers are always
involved in the game of business and that means either games of
strategy or of coalition. And even in coalition, there exists
group rationality only as long as the individual manager is better off in group cooperation. Thus competition always is the
sea upon which coalitions float. Consequently, we might suggest
that the same comments on the ethics of game competition apply
to oligopolistic games as for non-cooperative games.

I will make four general comments on the ethics of game
competition and conclude with a principle.

(1) Certain game rules do seem to be elements in the practice of
business competition and, as elements, these rules help concretize the patterns of responding to persons within this horizon.
Insofar forth, these rules function as do cultural patterns and
the ethician hesitates to judge them without sympathy (in business as a system). One must attend to what good persons in business think are the ethically acceptable practices. By "good

persons" I indicate those whom one may admire and whose opinion
one respects because of personal acquaintance or because they
particularly have impressed one in public thoughtful behavior.
Of course, one can be fooled here, but, in the long run, the
judgment of those who in business are concerned with acting as
good persons in business is the concrete standard one has to
work with and from which reflective ethical principles specific
to business most often are drawn.

(2) To approach business competition with the analogy of a game
entails that the justice involved within the competition horizon
(business as a system) will be independent of the end-results
and a matter only of fair processes. Thus, competition cannot
be justicized as a practice by the demand that all those involved and affected get what they deserve. The outcome of the
competition is not ever simply a matter of merit, talent, or
effort. F. A. Hayek testifies that this "pure process" concept
of justice in business developed in the late sixteenth century
and early seventeenth century after the schoolmen abandoned the
effort to discover "just prices" and "just wages" in the devel-
oping economic system and turned to hold that justice was ob-
tained in the prices and wages determined by just conduct of the
people engaged in market competition, that is, the conduct which
abstained from fraud, monopoly, and violence.[32]

(3) Competitors, customers and the public at large have prima
facie rights (e.g., safety) which transcend the legitimate field
of business strategy (business as a subsystem). Just what these
rights may determine about decisions in any business situation
cannot be prejudged, but the mere acknowledgment of their possible priority suffices. Otherwise we enter the world where
there are no rights except to use what power one has to survive
and to thrive, indicated by the animal terminology of "rat race,"
"squirrel cage," and "jungle."

(4) These decisions in business give us a prime example of an
area where one who tries to be a good person must weigh the possible as well as the ideal in the decision. Business is a long
term process, and the attempt to correct what one judges to be
an unethical procedure often must itself be a long term process.
Hence, individual acts in the sequential process may fall short
of an ideal but remain the reasonable decisions along the way.
Conversely, if one chooses the ordinary long term method to modify unethicality, one runs a danger of rationalization or eventual self-compromise. To guard against this, one must articulate
the long range goal of the correction of an unethical practice,
and also articulate exactly how the sequential process should
lead to the long range correction. This itself is only good
business procedure.

(5) Finally, I suggest again the principle used to guide one in

a context of secondary horizons: to realize a right (for example: to earn a living in the most commodious way) one may use
secondary horizons for the interpretation of acts (here: business strategy) as long as such interpretation acknowledges any
possible context shared with higher, possibly conflicting rights
interpreted by the primary ethical horizon.

VIII. Emulation: The Spirit of Competition

Before we turn specifically to the third part of the ethics
of business competition, we need to reflect briefly on the spirit
of competition as we find it in our society. To do this, I suggest a look at competition in those games we usually surname as
"sports" or "athletics." I suggest further an arbitrary restriction on the use of the two surnames. Persons can engage in games
such as baseball, football, field hockey, and the like for two
radically different purposes and with two radically different
measures to judge procedures. The "ethics of competition" for
the two styles of game would differ. For discussion, let us
designate them in the following manner.

Athletics: purpose of those who engage therein = victory
            measure to judge procedures in game = any means to
               desired end. (Obviously, a procedure for which
               one is liable to penalty is ambivalent, and to
               be used only if the percentage is on the side of
               achievable value and not the received penalty.)

Sports: purpose of those who engage therein = excellence
               in performance in game against opponent
            measure to judge procedures in game = fairness of
               initial situation; expression of ability and
               effort in acts according to rules.

The satisfaction one gains from engagement in these games
has two sources: (1) the practice of the game, from which are derived the rules for actions and the meaning of actions as well
as the ideal for actions in the play of the game; and (2) the
competition itself, from which is derived the challenge to act
for the purpose of the game. In sports, satisfaction comes with
excellence in performance; in athletics, with victory. Thus the
very notion of competition and the experience of it differ as a
function of satisfaction in the two styles of game play. In
athletics, it is a condition or a means. In sports, it is an
essential part of the goal itself, but not the entire goal.

The argument as to which purpose and which measure for procedures is of primary importance in the games of baseball, football, field hockey, and the like, still goes on. But the very
existence of the dispute suggests that the distinction between
"athletics" and "sports" is valid. Satisfaction seems obtainable

from either kind of game attitude---to achieve satisfaction from
victory over opponents or to achieve satisfaction from excellence
in performance in the game against an opponent. Even from "professionals," we have reports of an experienced richness in any
excellence of performance in true competition that simply is not
available in victory alone.[33] Certainly, "to win" is part of
the practice of such games, and even in sports there is excellence in performance only in terms of the meaning of the actions,
and this meaning from the practice ultimately derives from the
goals of the game, which include victory. However, in sports it
is the excellence in performance with ability and effort in the
game against an opponent that is more crucial for participants,
and constitutes a value higher than victory itself. And this
controls the ethic of the person in competitive sports. According to the Aristotelian principle, to act with one's capacities
in itself is pleasurable. To act excellently is most pleasurable, for then one is challenged to be fully in act. In sports,
the game sets up the specifications for what is "excellent," and
the best games require most in excellent performance.

The ethic of the person in competitive athletics is otherwise. The athlete will not hesitate to use procedures other
than those derivative from the practice of the game itself to
bolster chances for victory. One major class of such other items
is "psychological warfare," i.e., doing actions not derivative
from the game practice, but which actions are not forbidden by
the rules and which tend to upset the opponent's own excellence
of performance efforts. The person in competitive sports would
not be interested in such because of the very purpose sought in
engaging in a game as a sport.

When the ordinary person hears the word "competition," that
person thinks of individuals or teams competing against each other in games such as athletics or sports. The ordinary person
thinks of individuals or teams which strive to perform better
than opponents, or who try to gain an advantage by doing something slightly different than opponents.

One notes that in business competition, the traditional
sense of competition in classical economics is otherwise. Such
a classical concept imagined price as the basis of maneuvers,
and competition to be that situation where there is such equilibrium that each player knows that the best action is not to
try to achieve something in any way other or better than that
done by opponents in the industry. To view competition thusly
as an equilibrium situation came from Cournot and it has domi-
nated the economic thought until recently. But F. A. Hayek and
P. J. McNulty point out that originally in English economic
theory competition was not a situation but an active process.[34]

Competition as process admits the factor of management while

competition as situation does not. As process, competition can
go on even in cooperative games because it could be only for the
time being that strategy of individual rationality may not be as
beneficial as coalition. Managerial competition as process can
thus include coalition as a special case.

Thus there is equilibrium as well as disequilibrium competition, and the ordinary person's concept of competition may
after all be at the heart of business competition. This suggestion seems consonant with the thought of Joseph Schumpeter
who writes of the "perennial gale of creative destruction" where
competition comes from the threat or the fact of introduction of
something new into the industry: a new commodity, a new technology, a new source of supply, a new kind of organization.[35]

The manager competes by (1)the ability to break out from
routine; (2)the ability to sublimate existing structures that
serve the existing circular flow and equilibrium; (3)the ability
to see the potentials present in the given situation but which
potentials carry the contradiction of the given situation.

Just as the sportsperson and the athlete, the manager gains
satisfaction in competition, and the manager can gain it primarily (as the sportsperson) in performance, or primarily (as the
athlete) in victory.   In The Gamesman, Michael Maccoby analyzes
the variant meanings for performance and victory by today's managers.[36]

But one cannot presume a transfer of the ethics of competition from sports and athletics to business, especially in respect
to the ethics of seeking satisfaction from emulation itself. To
do this, we must move on to the third part of this investigation
as structured by Dr. Frank Knight.

IX.   (C)   The Business Game and Society

The modern idea of enjoyment as well as of achievement has
come to consist chiefly in keeping up with or getting ahead
of other people in a rivalry for things about whose significance, beyond furnishing objectives for the competition,
little question is asked.[37]

If the spirit of competition so permeates our thinking in business and many other dimensions of our society, and if business
competition is a major contributing source which makes "emulation and rivalry the outstanding quality in the character of the
Western peoples," the ethician must question competition as a
motive in relation to the fundamental ethical horizon. We here
will ask two questions: what does competition do to society?
and, what alternatives does society have to fill whatever need
it has that competition now fills?

(1) What does competition do to society? Basically it fosters a social atmosphere in which there is always some reward
schedule for performance or for status achieved and displayed.
Originally society refused to allow some areas to enter the competition arena or refused to allow some areas to be taken into
the business market. For example, the school system. Because
of some value, society did not want such areas to be affected
by competition guided by individual or by group rationality.
Society wanted these areas to be guided solely by societal system rationality. Recall, that in game theory, competition in
group rationality or in societal rationality makes them always
unstable and special cases of individual rationality. By re-
moving such areas as the school system from competitive arenas,
society said that societal system rationality was to be stable
and primary in such matters. (We note ironically that those who
participate in the school system have justified the use of competition in the classroom for grades, etc., "to get students
ready for the real world.")

If competition fosters a social atmosphere in which there
is always some reward schedule, the ethician must question: is
this a way to specify the principle of rational social cooperation?

According to the principle of process justice, a reward
schedule could be justicized if the start of the competition
were fair, that is, if there was the kind of situation to which
persons who are self-ordering individuals could agree. The persons would be willing to set up such a procedural system at such
a starting situation of fairness even if they did not know what
part they would take. If such conditions would be conceivable,
we could talk about process justice in the matter of competition
within society according to some schedule of rewards for performance or for status achieved and displayed. There could be justice even without equality in the results from the process.

But the difficult matter for process justice is the beginning situation. Here we face one of the great disputes of our
day. There is great dispute as to what kind of equality and
how much equality must be in a social situation before the performance of individuals begins in order to reflect the fairness
demanded by individual dignity. Thus this is the crux of the
justicization of competition in a society which stresses competitively set reward schedules. To judge the justice of what one
has in a society, one must have some principles by which to
judge initial engagement with a society's institutions. "What
one deserves" can be ascertained from the reward schedules of
the institutions according to the set practices thereof. But
whether or not what one deserves is ethically satisfactory cannot be ascertained except by reference to the fairness of the
start.

(2) What alternatives? Certainly competition presents us
with a mechanism for distribution of rewards. In addition, competition so permeates the many dimensions of our society that
one must conclude that the spirit of emulation and rivalry fills
a basic need in persons in society. Dr. Knight suggested that
competition's key offering was that it made our activities "interesting."[38] No matter what the game, no matter what the result, the very fact that the game has competition makes it more
interesting. Sometimes this is disguised by a statement that
the game has "incentive for effort." This theme raises the ambiguity again between "athletics" and "sports." No matter. It
is the interest supplied by competition that we need.

William James wrote an essay entitled "The Moral Equivalent
of War" in which he said that pacifism would never succeed until
there was found a substitute for that function which the call to
war precipitates in a sluggish and flaccid society. War, for a
lethargic time, is a tocsin to such disciplinary effort that a
people rejuvinates its interest in social cohesion.

I submit that one has no case against competition without
"a moral equivalent of competition." That I would call for a
moral equivalent of competition says nothing more than that
which those who have delved into the game theory say: at bottom,
poker, business, and war are all games which interest us out of
an otherwise dull, sluggish, and flaccid atexia of "real life
without a plot." We need an equivalent of competition because
of its positive effects in our lives.

But there is an ethical demand for an equivalent that is
other than competition as we have it today, for it has also a
negative effect that is also with us. Competition today and the
stimulus of interest which comes with it suggests a little too
much that "success makes right." The ethician would rather have
a radical separation between might and right, between power and
right, between success and right. After all, interested activity alone is not quite all there is to make a life significant,
for there are different kinds of activities that interest us.
Life must be exciting to be worthwhile and significant. But
not all that makes for excitement are humanly or ethically
equivalent.[39]

CHAPTER SIX

ETHICS AND POWER

The two most primeval phenomena of human experience are love and power, and neither totally yields to rational discourse. Since the rise of specifically-directed human love between individuals, which comes on the scene for the first time anywhere in the West in the Eleventh century, much has been written on love. And since the Renaissance, a fair amount has been written on power. This especially is true of our present century.

I will first simply give examples of where we find the phenomenon of power. In a society, there is power exercised between individuals: parent-child; lawyer-witnesses; dean (teacher)-students. There is also institutional power. The government has power to levy taxes, to enact and enforce laws, to control release of information, to lead the country to war, to decide to build public highways instead of public rapid transit systems. The media have power to select what to report, to select the order of what is reported, to give tone to what is reported by spacing and conjunction.

We are most interested in this work in corporational power. Since there are many manifestations of this power, I here will simply list a few.[1]

a) Power to determine the when, where, and how of its operations.
b) Power to determine the product and its quality.
c) Power to administer prices (a capacity significant under an oligopolistic control). One important byproduct is the power to form new capital with part of the price, a power absent in any pure competition system.
d) Power to coordinate and integrate the flow of goods and services.
e) Power to give or withhold dividends.
f) Power to induce consumption and sales through advertising.
g) Power to aim the majority of private research.
h) Power to hire and to fire.
i) Power to affect the lives of "corporate wives."
j) Power to sponsor entertainment on radio and TV media.

A. A. Berle has written that power, as far as it carries, is always absolute. It may be limited in scope, but that is a different thing altogether. Within the limitation of the field of power, those who have it, and Berle speaks of the business managers of our time, "act in their 'discretion'---which is merely a lawyer's way of saying that their power is uncontrolled."[2]

Americans have been ambivalent in their evaluation of power. We expect good people to use power to further worthy progress. We insist that all use of power be guided by rules of fairness and sensitivity. And yet we fear power as corrupting those who have it and destroying the freedom of those subject to it.[3] We must examine it carefully as it exists in business.

I. Analyses and Descriptions of Power

The ability to change reality is a potentiality and a need in each human person. And to act in accord with this potentiality and need is to exercise power in the most general sense.[4] Effective self-ordering thus is identical with power in this general sense. Each act one does changes the concrete situation including oneself and one's relationships so that the situation can never again be the same.

John Locke suggested that the rudimentary content for our idea of "power" comes from our observation of our abilities to affect our immediate situation. "Observing in ourselves, that we can at pleasure move several parts of our body which were at rest."[5] Sigmund Freud has consciousness distinguish the ego and the external world in terms of what one has power over, and what one does not. The child "must be very strongly impressed by the fact that some sources of excitation. . . can provide him with sensations at any moment, whereas other sources evade him from time to time."[6] Thomas Hobbes noted well that the exercise of this general capacity for power is a basic need in persons. "So that in the first place, I put for a general inclination of all mankind, a perpetual and restless desire of power after power, that ceases only in death."[7]

One might say from such comments that the enjoyment of the exercise of power amidst social intercourse is rudimentary in persons and needs no external explanation or goal for its intelligibility. The exercise of power brings its own enjoyment and intrinsic meaningfulness to the one who acts. Besides this intuitive concurrence that the exercise of power in the individual carries its own meaningfulness, there has also been an intuition that the acquisition of power was positively significant for the social group. William Wordsworth wrote:[8]

The creatures, see, of flood and field,
And those that travel on the wind---
With them no strife can last; they live
    In peace, and peace of mind.

For why? Because the good old rule
Sufficeth them, the simple plan,
That they should take, who have the power,
    And they should keep who can.

This intuition, that there can be no vacuum of power in a well-ordered society, has its most familiar expression in Thucydides. The Athenians, in 416 B.C., sent ambassadors to the island of Melos to negotiate (by talk or force) a takeover of political control. The envoys, writes Thucydides, gave this statement:

> Our opinion of the gods and our knowledge of men lead us to the conclusion that it is a general and necessary law of nature to rule wherever one can. This is not a law we Athenians made ourselves, nor are we the first to act upon it since its establishment. We found it already in existence, and we shall leave it in existence for ever among those who come after us. We are merely acting in accordance with it, and we know that you or anybody else with the same power as that which is now ours would act in exactly the same way.[9]

There have been many descriptions of power in our own time. Keeping the intuitions of the past in mind, let us analyze the elements in some contemporary studies of power.

Bertrand Russell defines power as "the production of intended effects."[10] This is a very simple and brief definition, and it keeps in suspension the various kinds and loci of effects.

Goldhamer and Shils write that "A person may be said to have power to the extent that he influences the behavior of others in accordance with his own intentions."[11] This suggestion brings in the element of a relationship to others by the one exercising power, and the influence by the exercise of power on the behavior of others. The influence can be physical, by explicit ordering, or by implicit manipulation.

A third description, by Arthur S. Miller, explicates another aspect. Miller first sets up the relationship between power and decision-making. Then he defines power as "the ability or capacity to make decisions affecting the values of others, the ability or capacity to impose deprivation and to bestow rewards so as to control the behavior of others."[12] Miller adds the element that to affect the behavior of others is to enter into the lives of others in terms of their values, and he adds the element that the mechanics of power are in terms of the production of sanctions. Power is seen to fail unless there is some sanction if the one to be subordinated resists the exercise of the power. This sanction can be either in terms of the removal of a value already possessed or the obstruction to the attainment of a value. Thus the sanction, which is the mechanics of the exercise of power in an interpersonal relationship, functions as the control by the powerwielder over the vulnerable relationship that exists between the one to be subordinated and values.

For a description of power in a business corporation, we

must include the aspect of social power that comes through organization. Organization is described by A. A. Berle as "the mechanism by which the decisions and instructions of a central individual or group can be made causative at distant points of application."[13] The significant element here is that, in a society, organization generates a logarithmic increase in power (organization powers power).

Finally, Carl Kaysen writes:

> The power of any actor on the social stage I define as the scope of significant choice open to him. Accordingly, his power over others is the scope of his choices which affect them significantly. . . .(This idea of power) is appropriate to a social system in which we see human actors, individually or in organized groups, as facing alternative courses of action, the choice among which is not fully determined without reference to the actors themselves.[14]

With Kaysen's thoughts, we add one final item to the understanding of institutional power: the scope of significant choice open to power-wielders. The correlative result on the side of those subordinated by the exercise of such power is that individuals or groups in society have values and make decisions and do actions which would otherwise not be the case.

We might summarize here:

Business power is "the exercise of significant choice by person or persons expressed through organizations which results in control by means of sanctions on values of the decisions and actions of others in respect to values, which decisions and actions these others would not otherwise make or do."

II. Some Useful Divisions on Kinds of Power

Power in a society may be looked at from two fundamental points of view, and each point of view has a primordial division in kinds of power. From the first viewpoint, the division is between "power to do things" (or "developmental" power) and "power over persons" (or "extractive" power).[15] From the second viewpoint, the division is between "private exercise of power in a society" and "public exercise of power in a society."

(1)The normal division of the expression of power into "power to do things" and "power over persons" relates to the difference in the immediate objects of the exercise of power. But in a society, the division often should be understood only in terms of the relative immediacy of the results of the power's exercise in respect to "power over persons." For every exercise of power changes the situation and all its relationships, and

the change of necessity must eventually reduce the control over
effects in society by others. This again refers to the determination of possible decisions and actions, or at least the determination of the scope of such, because of the exercise of
power.

This power is often difficult to measure. Individuals and
corporations usually affect the behavior and emotions of others
by means other than physical force or direct command. A method
of direct force or command only get the ones immediately subordinated to do something they do not immediately want to do.
David G. Winter writes, "Getting someone else to believe that
he really wants to do what you want him to do is surely a very
sophisticated technique for getting power."[16] Such would be
an example of manipulative power over persons.

In writing about power-to-do and power-over, C. B. Macpherson describes a distinction between "developmental power"
and "extractive power." By developmental power he means the
"ability to use and to develop one's capacities both as an individual and as a person in society." By extractive power he
means the "ability to use another person's capacities."[17]

How in a society does one gain extractive power? By the
use of sanctions. I deny another person access to what that
other person needs to exercise one's developmental power, and
I keep denying this unless that other person performs in such
and such a manner as I want. I thus get that other person to
do as I want as the condition for the other to gain access to
what the other wants in order that the other may exercise developmental power. This procedure Macpherson calls the "transfer
of power." For example, there is transfer of power within the
corporation for purposes of reward in terms of promotion, recognition, and salaries. There is transfer of power in the market
itself in the give and take of supply and demand, and transfer
of power in the interface between the market and the larger social system as business controls to some extent the wants and
satisfactions of members of social groups.

One might note well that it is an error to think that extractive power is apriori an impediment to developmental power.
It may be, but it need not be. Also to note is that extractive
power transfer is not a relationship that can be described as a
"zero-sum game." A zero-sum game is a dynamic relationship
wherein as one gains there is an equivalent loss to the other in
the relationship. A zero-sum game description for the power
transfer situation would assume that there is a precise existing
quantity of power that is the resource in society. This is
false, for it ignores the side of developmental power. If one,
in dynamic interaction in a society, increases knowledge, skill,
and the ability to perform acts (say, through technology), then

one's developmental power increases. And, of course, the sum
of possible extractive power also increases.

Now why do we think that the corporation today presents us
with a new problem in the exercise of power? Here are two quo-
tations to give us a feeling of the present situation.

Peter Drucker writes:

> What we look for in analyzing American society is...the in-
> stitution which sets the standard for the way of life and
> the mode of living of our citizens; which leads, molds, and
> directs; which determines our perspective on our own soc-
> iety; around which crystallize our social problems and to
> which we look for their solution. What is essential in soc-
> iety is...the dynamic element...the symbol through which
> the facts are organized in a social pattern....And this, in
> our society today, is the large corporation.[18]

Abram Chayes writes:

> ...the ability to control, within relatively broad limits,
> the price and quality of products made and offered for sale.
> This is traditional market power....Economic power is not
> the whole story, however, nor perhaps even its most impor-
> tant part. Concern with the modern corporation is inten-
> sified to the extent that its activities have necessarily
> ramified beyond the economic sphere....Across a widening
> range of activity, the large corporations have become
> principal factors.[19]

What has taken place, according to many readers of American society, is that the large corporations have moved to the very center of our social system. Their organizational operations give
the tone to the society, as well as control the major portion
of its economic existence.

Consequently, the two ethical question pertinent here are:
how does this power-over of corporations affect developmental
power; and, how does one legitimate the specific power holders.

Before we leave this introductory section, I must make a
few comments to warn against oversimplification. "Power over"
is ethically ambivalent. Its exercise brings about the situations within which persons act and out of which certain possibilities for action arise. We today are more sensitive to how
interactions and interrelations between persons and groups both
curtail and promote new developmental activities. One the positive side, we know that specification and order amidst the
range of future possibilities, even if such specification and
order come from "outside," are vital if persons are to summon

and focus their free energies to exercise freely their capacities to the fullest. Evidence for this is the enjoyment of successful response to proportionate challenge in sports with explicit rules.

On the negative side (though not necessarily ethically negative) is that the exercise of power in a society brings a reduction for those affected in the range of personal alternatives
those affected henceforth enjoy, and often enough also an increase in dependence on the power's exercise. Thus, "power
over" in a society can be said to determine to some extent the
factual values for persons affected by its exercise.

The human person desires self-expression (self-ordering,
expression of developmental power through exercise of capacities) because it is in such that one experiences significance-
for-oneself of living at all. This is the bedrock of value in
life from which all other values seem derivative. And yet it
is within the situations created by others that one expresses
oneself and finds specification for expression. Thereby, the
others insofar forth determine the "heritage" which consciousness "takes over" and one's self-expression also expresses
these others.[20]

Even with these qualifications, the two ethical questions
above remain, and we will take them up below.

(2)The second viewpoint on power gives us the division between "private power" and "public power."

Let us first recall our resultant description of business
power. Business power is "the exercise of significant choice
by person or persons expressed through organizations which results in control by means of sanctions on values of the decisions and actions of others in respect to values, which decisions and actions these others would not otherwise make or do."
Within a corporational structure today, the managers have a
"scope of significant choice" open to them that widely and significantly affects the determinations of how others within and
without the corporational structure experience and express human
values. These corporational managers, by the mechanism of the
organizations, make decisions that are causative at distant
points of application, both inside and outside the individual
organization.

As society's organizations become more complex, they become
more interlaced and thereby more counterbalanced in their scope
of initiative action. For example, where there is an oligopoly
in a particular economic area, the corporations therein find it,
from various causes, more beneficial according to the economic
horizon, to counterbalance each other in terms of "long range

considerations" that usually run parallel to each other rather than in terms of conflict. Harmony on price, the key issue in classical economics, has proven to be more beneficial in the oligopolistic situation for the corporations. Therefore, the harmony demand evinces a counterbalance in initiative among the managers. For the scope of initiative is set within boundaries that preclude the uncertainties for the managers of classical economies.

This initiative counterbalance, however, brings about an important consequence in the society. As organizations find the scope of their initiative action lessened by the oligopolistic phenomena of a few large corporations dominant in a given economic area, there is a reduction of any counterbalancing in the consequent effects of the actions of these corporations in the social arena. This is an important consequence in any analysis of social power. Let us reflect why.

If anyone subject to a function of organizational power is still ultimately free to disassociate oneself from the subordination to the exercise of that power, with some but with no drastic repercussions in one's total life, then the "power over" to which that person is subordinated may be said to be private power. Such a freedom of the one subjected to the "private power over" presupposes that there are other significantly distinct sources whereby one can have access to those items needed for the exercise of "power to do things" (developmental power) and that these other significantly distinct sources produce real options for the one subjected to the "power over" at hand.

But if the disassociation, if possible at all, from one power source would be at best only to bring about the substitution of the one by another qualitatively the same source of "power over," then the "power over" may be said to be public power. When the consequent effect of the decision of one set of managers exercising power over persons can no longer be balanced out by decisions made by other managers of corporations exercising power over persons, then that power insofar forth ethically is considered to be public social power. And the ethical justification of this power will be qualitatively different from the justification of private social power.

III. The Ethical Legitimacy of Social Power

One must question power that can make things happen in respect to basic values in a society and ask if it is legitimate. The question is raised today for non-owned economic organizations and especially is critical for all organizations which by the interlacing of society have had their power effects take on the "public" quality noted above.

Power is a fact, but the persons concerned can ask for the rationality of the title to its possession and to its use. By "legitimate" I signify that there are good answers in terms of human values to the questions "How come such and such has power" and "To what upshot does such and such have power." Such questions ask for standards by which to judge the possession and use of power, and apriori these standards are to be extraneous to the power itself.

In earlier times, the legitimacy of business power was allied to ownership of the capital items used in the process of corporational production. The owner, who was the head of the corporation, was quite like the owner proprietor of any small business today. Justification of the power of corporational business in such a system rested on the prior justification of private property itself, in the classical sense of private ownership of the means of production. This earlier world is no longer our world. But perhaps if we look more closely at the justification of the social power of corporations in these former times, we might uncover a clue to the question of legitimacy of managerial power today. For, as A. A. Berle points out, "In both cases, a question is raised---has been raised throughout all history. Why should this man or group of men hold power instead of some other group?"[21]

Berle follows this question with a principle in reference to legitimacy that seems to be rather generally acknowledged by those who recognize the question. "For the purpose of this study, 'legitimacy' is taken to mean merely that the holders of power are considered by the community to be justified in their tenure of it, and that the community considers the holders of property as justified in having it."[22]

The principle is that the power exercised in a society by the holders of large social power is ethically legitimate insofar as the public consensus accepts it. There is one initial drawback to this principle: it is merely formal. It does not state what is the object of the consensus, nor does it explain why this principle is the procedure for justification. So its mere formality needs help in two directions.

To the second, the "why" of public consensus is based upon what the power under discussion is---power that affects those in society beyond the business system. Thus, an appeal to "the principle of free association" is inadequate. Only the concession appeal is operative here and concession is expressed both in law and in public acceptance.

To the first, the "object" of public consensus, we refer again to Berle. No matter what the power in society, be it governmental or corporational, it is considered ethically justified

by the public if it fulfills two criteria: (1)it is acquired in
a customary form, by some established ritual; and (2)it performs
acceptably a more or less defined function.

Managers given token acknowledgment to the first as they
undergo each year a ritual stockholder vote. The second criterion would hold that managers of large corporations are ethically
justified in the exercise of their social power if they run
their operation in accordance with the expectations of the society. This criterion is not to resolve the question whether
corporations exist by concession from society or by inherence
from the right of free association in all persons, or the question which of the two is more basic. At issue here is the right
to exercise massive social power. Abram Chayes underlines the
social concern:[23]

> It is implicit in the ideal, as here defined, that the pro-
> cesses and institutions of the society be organized so as
> to give reasonable assurance that significant power will
> be exercised not arbitrarily, but in a manner that can be
> rationally related to the legitimate purposes of the
> society.

What is the basis for this requirement? What is the presupposition that supports the demand that corporations function with
their objectives convergent to the legitimate purposes of society? Actually, there are at least three presuppositions.

> (1)The corporational members of the business enterprise
>   form a subsystem within the larger social system.
> (2)All legitimate power in a social system rationally
>   relates to the purposes of the social system.
> (3)All subsystems function legitimately in the social
>   system only insofar as their effects within the total
>   system in general pragmatically work for the benefit
>   of the total social system, or at least not to its
>   detriment.

Illegitimate power, consequently, would be power in an institution which does not acknowledge this standard for legitimacy extrinsic to the power itself, and extrinsic to the subsystem in
which it originates. Without such an extrinsic standard, there
is no socially acceptable criterion to decide whether or not
those who use the power are using it in conformity with some
rational purpose which must be there to justify any institutional power within society.

The question, how well does the business enterprise fill
that function wherein its purposes converge with the legitimate
purposes of society, might be approached from two directions.
First, we might approach it in terms of the conceptions by those

in business of what their corporation is doing as a factor in
the economic subsystem. How well do these conceptions relate
to what is deemed needed from business by public consensus?
This is a constantly relevant question for, even if the relation
is ideally consonant at one time, new situations may break the
consonancy. And it is a commonplace today that there are new
demands made on business because of the generally kaleidoscopic
as well as ever more rapid series of changes that occur throughout the entire social system.

Peter Drucker writes of four fundamental discontinuities
germane here: (1)new technologies which have major effects on
society as well as on business (e.g., the computer); (2)the global shopping center, where there is a world economy and multinational corporations, but no non-economic institution suitable
to function in the situation; (3)a new pluralism, that is, a
pluralism of institutional diversity and diffusion of new power
in society in which every single social task of importance is
entrusted to a large institution; and (4)most important of all,
the passing of experienced-based institutions and their replace-
ment by knowledge-based institutions in which the systematic
acquisition of knowledge is the foundation of performance.[24]

So far the conceptions of those in business in this time
of the "rapidation of discontinuity" are responding to the call
for social convergence along the lines suggested by Max Weber.
Weber concluded that legitimacy of social power correlated with
the conviction on the part of those subject to the power that
such power was "inevitable,""reasonable," and "in the ultimate
interests of all." Businesspersons today consider it their task
to convince the public at large that business power is inevitable in this age wherein governments are too sluggish or too
bound by nationalistic prejudices to be able to respond to rapid
changes. They must convince the public that business power is
rational and in the interests of all by appeal to their skill
and performance in management (perhaps by contrast to those in
government). They know the goals and they know the means to
these goals, and they alone have the managerial expertise. By
these efforts, they support their claim their power is legitimate.

With respect to this first approach to how well the business function finds its purposes converge with the legitimate
purposes of society, i.e., what those in business think they are
doing in this regard, C. B. Macpherson makes some interesting
observations.[25] In summary his position is as follows. The
democratic business society has justified itself in general with
the claim to maximize two goals. It claims to maximize human
utilities, that is, the satisfaction of human desires; and it
claims to maximize human power, that is, developmental power.
These two claims, however, make up an ambivalent perspective on

human nature. The former views the nature of the human person as a "bundle of appetites" which seeks satisfaction. The latter views the nature of the human person as that of a doer, a creator, and an enjoyer of the exercise of one's abilities, which view John Rawls calls the Aristotelian principle for understanding human values.[26]

From Aristotle to the seventeenth century, generally speaking, the human person was conceived to be one who was happy if acting by a rational principle in any performance wherein one engaged one's human capacities. With the emergence of the modern market society, there was a shift to the conception in which that person was happy who was able to satisfy the appetites to consume items. The person was still considered a rational being, but rational behavior henceforth was action toward unlimited individual appropriation as the means to satisfy one's unlimited utility quests. The classical "economic person" was the new model of the rational person.

Thereby was gained a justification for market transfer of power as the way to gain utilities. Thomas Hobbes could describe power in this context as "the present means to obtain some future apparent good." Power was considered as a means extrinsic to some acquisitive goal human beings had.

In the nineteenth century, J. S. Mill combined the two viewpoints with his emphasis on individualistic liberty. He saw the market society not only compatible with individualistic liberty, but the place wherein one best could exercise individualistic liberty.

In the twentieth century, the concept of business society as the maximizer of utilities has been abandoned. Primarily there was a logical problem. The satisfaction that different people get cannot be compared by an observer. And so the aggregate satisfaction cannot be added together. Therefore, one cannot show that a given aggregate of utilities is more, or the maximum. Thus, one cannot show that a business society as we have it is a maximizer of utilities.

With these suggestions from Macpherson, we might now ask: if functions within the business horizon can no longer be justified as functions of a subsystem that serve a social purpose as a maximizer of utilities, can it still be justified in its social power as a servant of the social purpose to maximize developmental power? Perhaps the most promising way to respond to this question is to ask about the impediments that a business institution removes or places in the way of developmental power.

Still taking clues from Macpherson, we ask: what is the major impediment to developmental power? It is the "lack of

adequate means to life itself." Obviously here, we refer to
much more than physical subsistence. We refer even more directly to whatever is needed for an adequate psychic life. (Recall,
it is the intelligibly established value of human psychic life
that grounds ethical principles and gives ethical significance
even to physical life, and it is the experience of significance
is psychic goals and satisfactions that experientially grounds
human values.)Psychic life is a continuous stream of conscious
experience, and the actual values that each person and each society specify as ways to express their basic human self-ordering
vary with the diversities of the many streams of experience.

Perhaps the two most important implications for business
that come from these thoughts are: (1)many of the actual expectations result from cultural complexifications (Peter Drucker
suggests that in the U.S. today the car, for mobility, and the
TV, for instant information visually available, are psychic necessities!); (2)psychic value expectations relate to a primary
factor in economic theory---scarcity. Much of scarcity in society is relative, relative to how persons in society are conditioned to interpret the actual needs in their lives for development as human persons. Since we no longer accept the justification of corporational activities as the supplier of the maximum of utilities, certainly we must conclude that the justification to use power to encourage more expectations and then to
meet these expectations can no longer be considered unlimited.

The second direction from which to approach the question of
how well the business institution finds its purpose converge
with the legitimate purposes of society would be to investigate
how the horizon for the interpretation of business activities
relates to the general horizon for interpreting the rights of
persons in society. How do the decisions and practices of the
managers affect the lives of people today as these people carry
out their quest for developmental self-ordering in society?
This will lead us into the question of "social responsibility"
taken in the next chapter.

IV.   Power without Property

Before passing forward to a look at the ethical justification of corporational power in terms of "social responsibility,"
I must insert here some comments in order that we might identify
just who we refer to that has power in corporational business.
For some, there is confusion introduced in the distinction between "Principal" and "Agent." As the agent is merely the
angel, the messenger, the representative of the principal, so
the thought goes, the agent really has no scope of choice but
to fulfill the interests of the principal. And that is the
agent's only ethical responsibility.

This formula presupposes the principal as the power-wielder, the agent as the instrument of power only. At best, this is a remnant of an age of property that is no longer the world of the modern business corporation. Berle sums it as follows:

> Property, theoretically considered, has two sets of attributes. On the one hand it can be a medium for creation and production and development. On the other it offers possibility for reception, enjoyment, and consumption....The twentieth-century corporation has proved to be the great instrumentality by which these two groups of property attributes have been separated one from the other.[27]

The earlier formula made the connection between property and power for two reasons. First, the two in fact were existentially connected. Property was the factual base of power to do things and power over persons. Second, the two in the eyes of the public were ethically connected. The owner of property not only did, but had the right to wield power in society. Perhaps those who still hang on to the "Principal-Agent" formula in talk of the large corporational business firm of today really are seeking a facile justification for the use of power by appeal to simplier times.

In contrast to the simpler times, more and more observers are now speaking of "power without property" or, for perhaps more ease in conceptualization, of an analogous "new property." In reference to our present society of corporations and other large institutions, for ethical purposes the two phrases "power without property" and "the new property" are equivalent.

The notion of "new property" is both simple and subtle, so let me briefly refine what lines of thought are involved.

Property in general may be described as a "socially acknowledged relation that a person has to what is considered, in the broadest sense, an item of value." Certainly, what is considered of value (except for subsistence in food, clothing, shelter) is to a great extent determined by the concrete attitudes within a cultural milieu. And what are the manifold ways in which, ordinarily understood, one may acquire relation to items of value are familiar to us all. And so we have our ordinary image of what we talk about when we say "property."

But this ordinary, common sense imagining is undermined by some significant socio-economic developments of the last sixty years. Many people today continue to be undisturbedly at ease with talk about property exclusively under the rubric of the individual's possession, use, and control of "permanent" and fixed items of value (real property) or of manipulable or consumable items of value (personal property). In fact, however,

with the growth of a corporate society, we now can argue that
this familiar rubric of property as real or personal has become
at least partially obsolete. Moreover, in terms of social power, the part where it is obsolete is the more important part.

One major indication of the need for a new rubric of property is that, in our society heavily toned by business relationships, political economists and business people themselves now
are willing to say that, for most of the large business corporations, there are capital investors, there are top and middle
managers, there are employees, customers, unions, the government, and the society at large that are related to the corporate organization, but there are no owners. That is, there are
none except the impersonal (albeit legal) entity of the corporation itself.

Let us look at this statement: there are no owners. Prior
to our century there were clearly owners of businesses, even of
large businesses. If there was stock (corporate securities),
such was held by only a few individuals in each company and usually in very large concentrations. Such holding of stock had
a purpose: ownership and control.

Obviously in our day such no longer is the case. (One million people do not own and control ITT.) This century we have
experienced what might be called dispersive financing. In the
great expansion, so much more capital was needed that many new
issues of stock were dispersed among many more people, and the
old corporations, with ownership and control through concentrated holdings, voluntarily or involuntarily, reduced in number.

Obviously also the purpose of stockholdings has also
changed. What is the purpose of stockholdings today, and how
does this affect the investigation of corporate power?

Most people today look upon ownership of stock, not in terms
of control, or even of ownership, of a company, but rather in
terms of a type of investment. For practical purposes, one may
say that, not only has ownership of large corporations passed
from an identification with those in control of power, but it
has passed completely out of existence. As investors, stockholders look to their holdings of stock as a method to return
interest on investment of their money. This is clearly the case
when we note that most investors broadcast their investments
around. It especially is noticable in terms of institutional
investors. By 1977, not only did 25 million people have direct
holdings of stock in listed corporations, but "institutions"
(especially insurance companies and banks) owned nearly 50 percent of the shares outstanding on the New York Stock Exchange,
and they accounted for nearly 70 percent of its trading volume
in shares.[28]

Given such phenomena, of what meaning today is reference to some "principal" in the control of the social power of corporations? As far as I can see, ethically there is little meaning.

Let us adopt Berle's phraseology here and call the stock investor a holder of "liquid property."[29] Formally, "liquid property" is that holding which the holder, by selling or borrowing on, can turn into money and do something different. For a property to be liquid, of course, it is necessary that the holder's only relation to it arise from the holder's capacity to transfer it.[30] Therefore, the result of stockholders today being more investors than controllers in corporations is that the stockholders are divorced from subjective relation to the underlying things constituting the productive mechanism of the economic dimension. In other words, as investors have their holdings convert more into liquid property, they are eliminated from significant control of corporations.

Significant control passes to others. Which others? The ones, again adopting Berle's phraseology, who have relationship to "operating property." This kind of property does involve a subjective relation to the mobilizing minds which make it operate, and it involves a relation to the "place an enterprise holds in the social-economic aggregate known as the United States."[31]

Thus the operating property has a double relationship that makes it special: a relationship to the experts who have the skill to "make it go," and a relationship to the socio-economic system within which it does go. This operating property means significant social power.

We have already noted that the large corporations today are in interaction of growing complexity with all the subsystems of society that we understand as institutions, especially government and education. The growth to complexity is one that has come not only vertically, in the divisions of an individual corporation, but also horizontally. And this horizontal growth has broken through corporational boundaries to interlace several corporations in oligopolistic ways, and also to interlace the entire business institution with government and education. Qualitative alterations have taken place in how and by whom social relationships are determined within the individual private organization, in the relations between the individual private organizations, and between these organizations, governmental bodies, and the social community itself. Corporational businesses today act with attention to the competitive market, but with more attention to a mutual self-interest of the leading businesses, or even at times with a mixture of this and "public interest." Government does not hesitate to curtail initiative from a "private" firm for the sake of "public interest," or,

conversely, to subsidize private sector business and education
for the "public interest," or to contract out to business and
to educational institutions some "public interest" undertaking.
Educational institutions concern themselves with good relations
with the business community and government for financial assistance, and with accreditation agencies for prestige.

In a society composed of such interlaced organizations, the
sharp distinctions between the public and the private sectors of
activities have faded. All members of society have been drawn
into new and manifold relations to all the organizations. This
means that those items of value, or wealth, which the individual
can have as "private possessory holdings" and "liquid property"
have become secondary in social significance.

From Locke to World War I in Anglo-American thought, these
items of private possessory holdings have been the key to civic
freedom, self-identity, and individual capacity to initiate effects in society. Now the socio-economic freedom, identity, and
initiative---in a word, the social power---of the private possessory holders are minimal. As a society we have entered an
era where the initiative comes from organizations, organizations
which act for organizational or for "public" interest. And the
"public" interest today means less and less each individual's
several interests and more and more primarily organized interests.

The relationship today that functions as wealth functioned
in the past is a new form of property whereby one has freedom,
identity, and initiative (=power) in society. This "new property" or this relationship to "operating property" one obtains in
a corporational social structure through the relationships one
has to various organizations. These relationships gain for one
a place in the interlaced socio-economic system of organizations. The new marriage of property and power is a union within
the blood line of the power structure itself, for the new property is itself this new power. One has this new property of
socio-economic place, or power status, insofar as one has ac-
tively functional relationships to the power systems. As active within the power systems, one individually has socio-economic power without the need for property in the traditional
sense of individual possessory holdings. One only needs to obtain a place, a status, in the organizational power systems.

Some kind of status in a community or in a private organization, of course, is nothing new. But the status now at issue
is no longer simply a social by-product of possessory holdings,
ancestry, or profession. The new status is a place of socio-
economic power within active organizational power systems.

In every activity within the corporate system, persons make

and express their selves as they transact with other persons.
Each one in deeds gives answers to those questions which either
are explicitly or at least implicitly in every personal encoun-
ter: "Who are you?" and "What do you mean for me?" The social
power that is the new property makes one respond in terms of
status and function: "I am one who has this place in the corporate society" and "I determine these values for you."

Usually in activities we express a functional connection
between some parts of ourselves and some parts of the supporting
socio-economic system. We are teachers, professors, administra-
tors at such and such an educational institution; we are experts
on this and are on such and such committees; we have such and
such training, such and such degrees, such and such projects to
our credit; thereby we are in such and such relationships to
this organization within the complex of interlaced organizations. That is "who we are."

By this part-functionality we conceptually merge a response
to "Who are you" with the response to "What do you do?" or even
more broadly "How do you fit into the socio-economic system?"
Thus when asked "Who are you?" or when we ask of others "Who is
that?" we really change the meaning of the question in our minds
and then employ functional categories "to handle" other persons
in our thoughts and to have identification as we are "handled"
in the thoughts of others. (We must be taught to do this. A
little girl at the border, when asked if she was an American,
replied, "No, my daddy is an American. I'm a girl.")

Generally, and perhaps especially in a "new property"
milieu, one's functional roles in the corporate society determine one's self-identity. And this identity is more and more
dependent upon the fate of one's immediate organization within
the corporate society, and upon one's acceptance by functional
peers and upon one's performance among functional inferiors.
Consequently, the primary concern of the person with "new property" must be organizational.

As holders of "new property," individuals exercise the
resultant social power to determine some relations that others
will have to the organization or to its products, and, thereby,
to the corporate society.

This shift in the connection between property and power,
especially when the power becomes "public," has some radical
implications for certain ethical categories of the past. With
an ethical vocabulary based on the old property rubrics, many
status power people still speak of these determinations they
bring about in the lives of others only in terms of privileges
or options or expediencies, and not in terms of rights and basic
human values. They thereby presume that to deny a relation to

the organization or to deny a criticism of its products is merely to deny a privilege or to deny the immediate enjoyment of
certain options or to deny that ethical categories are germane
to decisions of expediency. There is no wonder that universi-
ties, for example, still insist that students are there not by
right but by privilege. When organizations were private in respect to the power they wielded, such talk was more acceptable
ethically. But today, when organizations both decide upon and,
in their interlaced stance, supply those credentials which determine a person in the roles one has in the corporate society,
the subject's relation to them is now public and nearly or completely in the area of rights. As an example from business mar-
keting, if all major suppliers of certain food necessities so
package their goods and so modify the goods themselves through
processing that the ability of consumers to judge quality prior
to purchase is gone, then the exercise of a classical competition function by the consumers is denied by what is in fact an
exercise of public power by the suppliers. For there is no
reasonable substitute.

We are less and less a society of persons who receive entrance into "private" organizations by privilege or who use the
products of organizations by option.

V. Corporations and Personal Ethical Responsibility

We left off the matter of the legitimacy of power-wielding
in business corporations at the question of social responsibility because it was necessary to look at the new power that is
functional because of the interlaced organizations in society's
institutions today. Now there is a further problem: if a person is a holder of place in any organization within the business
institution, granted that the business institution and the individual corporation have new social power, does the individual
person have any real power as a person and, consequently, is the
person in an organization at all ethically responsible for the
effects in society brought about by the activities of the business corporation?

The corporation can be held legally culpable in our society
today. But is this legal entity, the corporation, the only real
item that in any sense can be "responsible"? This is not only
an ethical question of some import, it also alerts us to a very
real psychological tendency in persons: to feel free of ethical
responsibility in those decisions and activities wherein one is
but the agent of an organization.

This is not a valid attitude in ethics if we work with the
presupposed principle of legitimacy by means of public consensus. The reduction of all responsibility onto the entity named
"the corporation" is unrealistic. For the purposes of ethical

responsibility, the term "corporation" is but a shorthand de-
vice. What we really designate by the term "corporation" are
the top managers who decide company policy, and the layers of
managers who decide strategy, tactics or who implement such.
Thus, in a derivative way, the middle managers who must turn
policy decisions into operations are also, for ethical matters,
the "corporation." When U.S. Steel or General Motors makes a
decision, it means that some human beings have made a decision
and others will decide on strategy, tactics, and procedures to
carry it out. As with the analogous poker game, there indeed
is a buck and it does stop.

    This conviction is supported by the work and reflection of
A. A. Berle in his major work, Power.[32] Berle lists what he
terms "Five Natural Laws of Power." I offer comments on each.

(1) "Power invariably fills any vacuum in human organization."

    (a) In any choice between chaos and power, the latter al-
        ways is embraced by a society;
    (b) the principle here is that order in any social group is
        a felt need and thus bases the ethical legitimacy of
        the power to establish order;
    (c) thus the question of legitimacy ties in with the recog-
        nition and acceptance of social orderers;
    (d) consequently, the right to power of any kind is always
        a function of needed order in a society.

(2) "Power is inevitably personal."

    (a) To allude to a power class, a power elite, or "they" is
        to stop at abstractions for the sake of some superficial
        investigation of power itself;
    (b) power can only be exercised by decision and by the acts
        of an individual;
    (c) this does not deny that in an organization there can be
        a "sense" of the loss of exercise of initiative power.

(3) "Power is invariably based on a system of ideas (a phil-
    osophy)."

    (a) The people who work in and who accept from the outside
        any power organization must believe in what the organ-
        ization is trying to do;
    (b) this means they accept some idea system; this acceptance
        is indispensible. (One here recalls Machiavelli's prin-
        ciple: the prince must seem to act in accordance with
        the accepted notions of what it is good to do.)

(4) "Power is exercise through, and depends upon, institutions."

     (a) Otherwise, to wield power one must use physical force;

     (b) the organizations themselves are guided by ideas in their structures, and through them power is conferred and exercised at distances.

(5) "Power is invariably confronted, and acts in the presence of a field of responsibility."

     (a) Those affected by the power cannot but interest the one who wields the power;

     (b) unless those affected by the power are positive toward the power wielder, the latter must use physical force to keep the exercise of power, and thus the scope of power effects will be of necessity reduced;

     (c) insofar as those affected by the exercise of power are affected in areas of human rights, the power wielder is responsible ethically;

     (d) insofar as the organization, the institution, and the power are legitimized by public consensus in terms of the public good, the organization, institution, and the power are to be measured ethically in terms of values expressed in the consensus by that society.

We may conclude that there is no basis for an excuse that individuals have no individual power in corporations and are therefore in no way ethically responsible for the effects of corporational exercise of power in the society.

We might also draw a conclusion, at long last, about the ethical legitimacy of power in business corporations. The power wielders in the corporations must constantly validate the legitimacy of their power in society. Legitimacy today, by the nature of the new public nature of business power, is a process. The managers legitimize their power by competently performing a function which is needed and valued by whatever claimants to the accountability for values call reasonably upon business. The business managers have legitimacy of power as long as they serve claimants in ways that are satisfactory for reasonable human order in society. That is, they have legitimate power as long as they exercise the power they actually have (not the supposed power they may admit they have according to some dated model of business and economics) to good effects in society.

CHAPTER   SEVEN

THE SOCIAL RESPONSIBILITY OF BUSINESS

Responsibility is not the feeling of constraint, wherein I feel I must do a certain action. Rather it is the awareness of being-in-charge to some extent of things accomplished by my action in the situations that make up our world. It is the awareness that Harry Truman displayed with a motto on his presidential desk, "The Buck Stops Here." The buckeye knife used to designate the dealer in poker, the one who initiates a particular hand, stops somewhere. Responsibility is the awareness of capabilities for decisive assertion of my self in the temporal world with others, by which assertion I either justify myself or indict myself in some way measured by some standard for values.

When one acts responsibly, one exercises one's capabilities to change the way the world is. One's activities are causes in the development of this world. As such, one's activities are not distinguished from the transactions by any being in the temporal world, and are not distinctive of the moral experience. In technical terms, we locate the cause for the resultant novel situation in such transactions ("The weather ruined the picnic," "Joe knocked over the lamp"), but we do not attribute the unifying structure of the entire transaction to such non-moral causes. To attribute responsibility in the moral sense, we look for that degree of self-conscious self-ordering wherein a person initiates the order (ratio, reason) in the entire transaction for the sake of some valued goal. Thus, in our lived experience, moral responsibility is a function of being the initiator of the reason why a transaction takes place.

What in felt experience distinguishes the human person's activities from non-moral causes? Precisely that the person feels to some extent in charge of what will come about and what will be cut out in the emerging event (recall: a decision is both positive and negative, a "cutting off"). At least to some extent, one controls what transactions are, and one controls that they are.

The premises under which the subject of the social responsibility of managers in business arises are the following:

(a) economic transactions are transactions by human decision through organizations within a social world of persons;

(b) these transactions have (or could have) impact on values that are both economically understood values and values understood in

91

terms that are human but other than economic;

(c)those in control of such transactions are ethically accountable for the foreseeable consequences of such actions.

I. Subject Matter for Business Social Responsibility

The matters in investigation of the social responsibility
of business are the actions of power done by managers through
corporational structures. Questions on these matters arise
under two rubrics: what does business do to society, and what
could business do for society.

"Responsibility for what business does to society" involves
the impact in society which results from the operations proper
to the practice of business. This impact has two forms. (a)The
impact can be part of the operations (for example, product quality, product safety, and the social setting for the interactions
of all employees). (b)The impact also can be in unintended but
inescapable by-products of business operations (for example,
spillovers and externalities = costs associated with production
or consumption, which costs are shifted onto the community at
large and force the society's resources to be overallocated to
the production of the business's goods).

"Responsibility for what business could do for society" involves the possible actions by corporations in response to social problems which are dysfunctions of society but which dysfunctions are not considered to be effects of past business operations.

We must be somewhat careful as to what we presuppose in
this investigation. In other words, we must attend to horizons.
(By a horizon one orders facts, explains facts, sets up problems,
and restricts the kind of resolutions to problems that will be
appropriate. By horizons, one interprets what is at stake.)
For example, if we have the horizon wherein the corporation is
viewed as if it were only an example of person-to-person com-
merce writ large, we certainly would ask and judge in terms of
whether or not it were ethically good for me as an individual
to deal with my neighbor in such and such a way, and apply all
answers accordingly to the corporation. (If I simply deny myself a little in x area, my companion can improve his lot im-
mensely in y area. So I would be a cad, undeserving of human
respect, if I did not deny myself in x area. Likewise, the corporation.) We know from elementary economics that this is a
fallacy, perhaps the fallacy of composition.

Two horizons challenged by the concept of social responsibility are the horizon that restricts ethical values to interactions between individuals, and the horizon that interprets

the ethics of business decisions and activities by the play of
the "invisible hand" utilitarian convergence of business values
and social values. In these challenges, the concept of social
responsibility includes institutional activities in reference
to some set of values that we as a society acknowledge and to
some evidence available to all by which we can see these values
affected to some significant degree by the decisions and activities of large business corporations.

Since a society's basic value system is always vague and
seldom articulated except in cliches, some people deny that
there is any real set of values which all in the society do in
fact acknowledge. However, a consensus of some sort must function, for we have the experience both of some coordination of
diverse institutions and of certain minimum standards in behavioral codes.[1] More directly, one can draw up a reference list
with some minimum specification of such values. Here is what
A. A. Berle offered a few years ago.[2]

1. People are better off alive than dead.
2. People are better off healthy than sick.
3. People are better off literate than illiterate.
4. People are better off in beautiful than in ugly cities
   and towns.
5. People are better off adequately than inadequately
   housed.
6. People are better off if they have opportunity for en-
   joyment---music, literature, drama, and the arts.
7. Minimum resources for living should be available to all.
8. Leisure and access to green country should be a human
   experience available to everyone.

Such a list could certainly be extended or modified to some degree. (I might add, for example, "To deal with one another openly and justly is better than to deal with one another with un-
announced trickery.") But, as Berle points out, the ability to
draw up any such list refutes those who claim that to talk of
social values held in common is to talk nonsense or to talk private prejudices only.

Consequently, it is an ethical matter to query the activities of any institution that significantly does or could affect
such values or the ordinary means to such values. That phrase,
"the ordinary means," obviously is a working phrase. Few would
consider the institution ethically correct which directly acted
to deny persons the enjoyment of one of the values listed above.
But we must keep in mind that the enjoyment of values is a process event that comes after a series of other events. And to
interfere or to support the prior events which are considered
as the ordinary means to the eventual enjoyment of the consensus
value takes on ethical significance proportionately.

Still, there is no consensus on response to the question of the social responsibility of business. Let us examine some arguments that seem representative.

II. An Argument against Social Responsibility

Professor Milton Friedman's position is bluntly stated. As a manager in a business, the individual is directly responsible only to the owners of business. The extent of this responsibility is sharply defined, simply to "conduct the business in accord with (the owners' desires), which generally will be to make as much money as possible while conforming to the basic rules of the society, both those embodied in law and those embodied in custom."[3] As the agent for the principal (the "owner"), the manager is to run the business efficiently according to the economic model. As a businessperson, says Friedman, the manager has only this responsibility, and only this authority. But this behavior itself is good ethics, for the society is best served (the social utilitarian note) by a strong business institution, and this strength comes from managers who operate according to the "agent's" standard and the economic model.

Let us examine the steps in this position.

(1) <u>First Premise</u>. "The corporate manager is an agent of the owner in a free enterprise economic system."

(a) This premise presupposes a specific kind of relationship between manager and owner. The verification for the presupposition would be from two sources: law and traditional economic theory. There is an obscure connection between the two that lends strength to the verification. However, the social development in our century from "owners" to "investors" gives ethical ambiguity to the verification. And this ambiguity becomes more apparent as we note a second presupposition.

(b) The premise presupposes that the managers can identify the desires of the "owners." For the sake of argument, we might stipulate that Professor Friedman's statement of what generally could be assumed of the owners' desires was true some sixty years ago. But one might legitimately question whether this is the only desire for many investors today; namely, that the individual company make as much profit as possible. There is evidence to indicate that even the economic interests of the investors need different expression with the changing times. In a study by Henry C. Wallich and John J. McGowan, one sees that the diversification of the portfolio (the majority of stockholders today have diversified portfolios) changes the "interest" of those who hold stock in any individual business.[4] Thus, the very argument that the manager is obliged to the interest of the stockholder could be turned to support an obligation to trans-firm concerns. But this really is tangential, for it is up to investors primordially to care for their broader interests.

(c)This premise presupposes that one can sharply isolate the investors' profit interest from the owners' ethical interests, if these two differ. And it begs the question to assert that the economic standard for sound business is, for investors as investors, good ethics. That must be demonstrated by the argument, not presupposed behind a premise.

(d)The premise ignores the question of the social power of the business institution and who exercises this power. With power in the hands of managers and not the investors, simply to restate the "Principal-Agent" responsibility formula as the sole accountability line, would be to assert that managers are accountable to no one for what a corporation does to society by its proper operations. This is a gratuitous assertion and, as such, can be gratuitously denied. It is of no strength in ethical reflection.

(e)Finally, the premise presupposes an unethical attitude on the part of the "owners" (investors) in terms of their concern "to conform to the basic rules of society." To be consistent, Professor Friedman would only permit such conformity for the purpose of profits. Specifically, such conformity keeps the corporation and its managers out of costly court battles and keeps a minimum of good will for the corporation's public image. This would, of course, subsume potentially ethical values under the economic criterion for values.

((Comment on First Premise)) Since accountability for one's actions that affect others is the matter for ethical judgment, there can be little doubt here that the premise EQUATES good business values and good human values. The danger here is oversimplification. One does well to doubt the two are either equated or opposed. Actually, the relation suggested in the premise seems more a partim-partim matter (partly true, partly false). Certainly, to have the business institution flourishing in a society causes a better social situation than large unemployment and economic recession. Why? Rudimentarily, the subsistence needs of many people cannot be met without political aid during unemployment or recession. And this political activity is self-defeating over the long run. Yet since the meeting of the subsistence and human needs for developmental human activities is a social value, the means to such are indeed a primary social value. So we need flourishing business.

Yet it is an error to move from this to say, in addition, that anything that is good business is good social value. High tariffs may be good for business in the U.S., but this is not necessarily productive of social values. And in the other di-

rection, restriction of ugly billboards from highways, the prevention of suspected elements from entrance and accumulation in
ground and water and food cycles, or the prevention of suspected
elements entry into the open air and gradual accumulation in
human lungs may be good social values, but not necessarily good
economics.

(2) Second Premise. "To act with social responsibility as a
business manager implies to act other than in the interests of
owners."

Professor Friedman has a three-pronged argument for this
premise. If one would act with other than the economic standard
for evaluating one's business decisions, a manager would usurp
political power and perform inefficiently both economically and
socially. One would usurp political power, for one would employ
money that one had only agent power over, either money already
in hand or possible profits, as if one had principal power over
it. This is a form of taxation without representation and is
the usurpation of political power to which an economic manager
is not entitled. One would thus be economically inefficient,
for one would have foreign standards (i.e., political standards)
for the exercise of one's control over the money. And, finally,
one would be socially inefficient, for the manager has no specifically social expertise.

(a) Ironically, this premise and its argument presupposes a
model for the relation between business values and social values
that is other than the model that functions in the first premise. This presupposes a POLARITY relationship, wherein the
decision for social values by a business manager entails the re-
linquishment of good business practices, either by direct reduction of actual or possible profits, or by the attenuation of
efficiency in economic decisions. We sometimes hear this polarity presupposition spoken of in terms of the tension between the
"technico-economic must" and the "ethical ought," even by those
who do not agree with Professor Friedman's first premise.
Whether or not this polarity is ever true, one cannot simply assert that it is always true. And one, moreover, cannot assert
it with such terms that there is a weighting of the polarity;
namely, that since economic survival is the condition sine qua
non of social survival, and so of all other social activity,
then when it comes to a conflict, the ethical ought is the one
that always should give way. Even if at times there might be a
tension (which is stipulated here only for the sake of argument),
one has no basis to assert that in every potential economic-
ethical conflict, there is a matter of social survival itself!
So to phrase it as "must" versus "ought" is illicitly to expand
the principle "economic health is the necessary condition of
survival for all other values in society" to the principle "the
only way to survive is through efficiency in each and every

economic decision." This is accurate at most in the nearly perfect competition situation among small businesses. But there is
no strength in such an assumption for a large corporation that
operates in an oligopolistic situation with significant and
broadly reaching market power. At least, such an assumption
has no ethical force.

(b)A second presupposition behind this second premise is
the restriction on the "interests of the owners"(investors). We
have commented above on the changes that should be considered
because of the diversification of portfolios prevalent today.
But there is a further comment at this time.

One might agree that the investors wish profits. And the
manager normally functions in the managerial role guided by this
habitual wish, and probably is ethical insofar forth.

But the will of the stockholders can be assumed for our
study to be to do all things ethically well. (That is, we can
so assume if a basis for this study is that people want to act
ethically.) If the given corporate decision or policy, when
applied, would injure significant rights and values of persons
in society, the manager must judge that such a decision or policy in its effects would be against the ethical will of the investors, and the manager functions in their ethical interest
when the manager curtails such a decision or policy.

Obviously, the ethician must argue for a qualification of
the "interests" of the investors as stated in this premise, a
qualification in terms of the technique of horizons. To actu-
alize a right (e.g., to earn a living in the most proficient
manner), one may use intermediate horizons for the interpretation of actions (such as to act with an economic efficiency
standard) as long as such interpretation acknowledges any possible context shared with higher, possibly conflicting rights.
This must be a principle for ethics in business.

(c)A third presupposition behind this second premise is to
keep vague exactly what is included in the phrase "to act with
social responsibility." Professor Friedman seems to consider
all such actions in terms which call on business to modify its
pursuit of economic goals and take time, money, or expertise to
help society with some of its unsolved general problems (the
"what could business do for society" rubric). This dichotomy
of "economic goals---social problems" eliminates the investigation of the causes of some social problems. There may be
strength in Professor Friedman's position against business cur-
tailing its economic goals to take up general social problems
which are unconnected with its ordinary operations. But there
is little ethical basis for refusal to respond to social problems that arise from the ordinary operations of business itself.

(3) <u>Third Premise</u>. "To act with social responsibility as a guide instead of economic efficiency would mean the manager was to act other than in the interests of society itself."

(a)The main presupposition here is the danger to our society of the practices of socialism. For Professor Friedman, the socialistic principle relevant here is the principle that "political mechanisms, not market mechanisms, are the appropriate way to determine the allocation of scarce resources to alternative uses."[5] And since socialism has not yet proven to be a way for citizens to experience freedom, any practice of the socialist principle in economics is a threat to freedom.

Peter Drucker concurs (with a qualification noted below) and notes that this is not a denial of responsibility at all.[6] That business should stick to its business "is indeed the only consistent position in a free society. It can be argued with great force that any other position can only undermine and compromise a free society," because of the consequences studied in the second premise. To act with categories of social interest in one's decision is to usurp political power.

However, there is possibly a fallacy in the identification of social values which the call for social responsibility implies are to be operative in business decisions, and the socialistic political values. The fallacy becomes obvious when put in form.

A type of decision has B values (A entails B)

C type of decision has B values (C entails B)

Therefore, C type is equal to or identical with A type.

Just because a political horizon or a socialistic horizon may lead one to add social values to economic values in a decision process, it is a fallacy to conclude that anyone who so desires to add the social values is acting as a politician or as a socialist. This is the old fallacy that historically operated against Socrates. (Atheists question the gods; Socrates questions the gods; therefore, Socrates must be an atheist.) The technical name for this fallacy is the "Fallacy of the Undistributed Middle."

(b)A second presupposition for this third premise involves oversimplification. The argument assumes that the standard for interpretation of business decisions and policies must be either economic alone or social alone. That it could be the case that the ethical horizon for business is usually economic values (which most of the time could be argued to be consonant with social values), but that at times economic values and social values might conflict, at which times the ethical manager might

subordinate the one to the other---this possibility simply is
ignored. Drucker's qualifier is, "Yet Milton Friedman's 'pure'
position...is not tenable either. There are big, urgent, des-
perate problems....Business and the other institutions of our
society of organizations cannot be pure, however desirable that
may be."[7]

III. An Argument for Social Responsibility

There is still considerable ambivalence, confusion, and
resistance in respect to the cumbrous task of conjoining corporate ethical horizons to economic horizons. While most strug-
gle to integrate the demands they can hear, there is the very
understandable reaction by many managers to judge, evaluate, and
interpret the demands for social responsibility back into terms
of the traditional economic horizon itself. This translation
means the equation of good business and good ethics, or the
subordination of good ethics to good business, as means to
an end ("honesty is the best policy").

We might list briefly some expressions of this translation
of social responsibility by use of the traditional economic
horizon.

A.) S. R. is good P.R. Corporations have learned the economic value of good public relations and a good image for the
firm. Their image is a function of the actions of investors
and customers.

B.) S.R. is good long-term investment. The social environment contributes or discontributes to the success of the corporation. Corporations therefore want to contribute to that
environment for their operations which will favor the conduct
of their business. This will show up in specifics such as quality of the labor force, turnover and absenteeism, social crime
rate and property destruction, less taxes for public service
forces, etc.

C.) S.R. reduces the threat of government regulation.
Since regulation by the government is considered by corporations
as a potential restriction on the scope of their decision powers,
at least in those areas in which social responsibility discussion is most prevalent today, the corporation judges it expedient for its operations to satisfy the public call for social
responsibility in order to avoid government enforcement. ("The
government should let us alone and we will come up with our own
regulatory code.")

Insofar as these three translations are used to interpret
the social responsibility attitudes of managers, we see that the
ethical judgment on human developmental values ("social values")

are not primary. Economic values continue to control the process of decision. One critic notes the resultant phenomena that
such an attitude causes:[8]

> Business, in its daily conduct, reflects a disconcerting
> insensitivity to changing public demands and expectations.
> The lethargic response of the auto companies and of the
> oil companies to matters of pollution and safety are lead-
> ing examples. As contrasted to its leadership in technol-
> ogy, business's habits and conservatism dictate that it
> merely be responsive, and be dragged, heels dug in, into the
> new social values, rather than providing innovative leader-
> ship. Business responds in a piecemeal fashion and only to
> the critics who have enough power or enough nuisance value
> to enforce their demands.

This criticism recalls one of the major suggestions in reference
to the legitimization of power wielded in society by decision
makers in organizations: use of power in accordance with some
sort of public consensus. The companion suggestion was that the
power had to be exercised in service to the social system, that
is, as a means to the social weal. Since power in a free society ultimately resides in the persons who would agree to the
institutions which are the instruments of power, the people must
either themselves judge (by some sort of public consensus) or
authorize some specialists to judge the function of any social
power, especially such an enormous social power as that which
is the business subsystem in its dynamic processes.

Consequently, I have a serious suspicion toward the three
attitudes above which translate ethics into economics. For
these three attitudes to work, the corporation must succeed in
deceiving those who would judge the exercise of corporate power.
The institution would offer evidence to favor its own justification in the judgment of others and yet, as it does so, would
use its power to manipulate the judgment of its ethically appropriate evaluators. Doing this, instead of using its social
power in the social service, as a means to an end, it becomes
an end in itself, completely self-serving. And since it is the
use of power-over others, and not the absence of power-over others that bears the onus of proof of legitimacy, such a social
power is inadequately legitimized and insofar forth is unethical.

Because of our experience with the dynamism within the exercise of power, especially when power is exercised by those who
are to a significant extent unaccountable for their activities,
we have aposteriori reasons to demand some social checks and
balances on all significant business power. Ideally, no governmental regulations or departments would need be involved.
Those in business should be concerned enough that they discover

the consensus or lack of consensus on their own by some direct
survey of their various policies. Our experience, however, as
noted long ago by Thomas Hobbes, indicates that we all do our
ethical jobs better if we have that confidence in the performance of one another that comes from authoritative interpretation and enforcement of certain minimal behavioral standards.
But the argument here is that responsibility must be accepted
for social power because it is right that it be accepted, and
not that its acceptance will be enforced. This latter attitude
brings back the spectre of "anarchy with a policeman."

There are four terms in the social power relation: the power itself, the effects of the power, the standard for the legitimization of the power, and those who wield the power. It is
in the last term that the ethician locates the ethical responsibility and judges it to be there in proportion to how much
power each person exercises---from board directors, to executives, to middle managers.

> The demand of the law in a well-ordered society is that
> responsibility shall lie where the power of decision lies.
> Where that demand is met, men have a legal order, where it
> is not, they have only the illusion of one.[9]

> Stated in the form of a general relationship, social re-
> sponsibilities of businessmen arise from the amount of
> social power they have.[10]

> Each business has responsibilities in some way commen-
> surate with its powers.[11]

What these citations have in common is that each infers that
persons who have power must exercise a socially accountable control of that power, or else the exercise of power is ethically
illegitimate. This may be stated as a general ratio: there is
a proportionality between power and ethical responsibility. (I
will take up the reasoning behind this ratio in the next section.) Davis and Blomstrom have a most acute paragraph in which
they argue that there is surprising agreement that this ratio
is accurate.[12]

> The logic of reasonably balanced power and responsibility
> is often overlooked by those who object to social respon-
> sibilities for business. The fallacy of their objections
> is that usually they are based on an economic model of pure
> competition in which market forces leave business theoret-
> ically without any social power and, hence, no social re-
> sponsibility (a balanced zero equation). This zero equa-
> tion of no power and no responsibility is a proper theoret-
> ical model for pure competition, but it is theory only and

is inconsistent with the power realities of modern organizations. They possess such great initiative, economic assets, and power that their actions do have social effects.

This argues that those who deny social responsibility for business other than economic responsibility do two things at the
start; they accept a model of pure competition economics, and
they accept the principle that ethical responsibility goes with
social power! It is simply that they meld the model and the
principle together so as to find no social power other than economic power and so no social responsibility other than economic
responsibility.

I am not sure that Professor Friedman would accept this analysis of his position. But it is worth noting that he does not
hesitate to enter the fray of ethical evaluation. He does admit
that one can and should ethically evaluate the use of business
power, and insofar forth he acknowledges that the ethical horizon functions in the relation between the social system and
business as a subsystem. But he identifies the makeup of the
ethical horizon with the utilitarian model of social impact of
decisions from traditional economics.

Therefore, despite disagreement on social responsibility,
there seems to be a fundamental agreement that activities by
organizations within an institution in society should and do
undergo ethical evaluation. And there seems implicit agreement
that these organizations should and do undergo ethical evaluation in respect to what kind of power is exercised, who controls
the exercise, and what is the social effect of the exercise in
reference to values accepted in some overt social consensus.

The dispute centers over whether social responsibility is
identical with economic responsibility or not, and, if it is
not, does it involve what business could do for society as well
as what business does to society by its proper operations.

IV. Expressions of Social Responsibility

One of the first methods of response by those who gained
economic power in American business was philanthropy. It was
central in their interpretive horizon that God gave success to
those who had the talent, and that this success was a trustee-
ship for those who did not have the talent. Therefore, social
responsibility was an ethical obligation for those who were
economically advantaged to those who were economically disad-
vantaged. This latter could be the undersuccessful individual
or the underdeveloped social group.

The American philanthropists, such as Carnegie, gave huge
sums to individuals, schools, libraries, and the like, or set

up Foundations that would support worthy individual and social endeavors. The economically successful businessperson consider- ed this the method to carry out social responsibility. The principle was this: One's social responsibilities were to share with one's fellow human beings the bounty that came with one's particular talents.

Two items are of special significance in this principle: (1)the cause of social responsibility was economic success from the use of discriminative talents; (2)the receivers of acts of social responsibility were determined by standards unrelated to the exercise of the economic talents or the economic power.

According to the principle of social responsibility uncov- ered in the previous section, the matter is quite otherwise. (1b)The cause of social responsibility is the control of social power; (2b)the receivers of acts of social responsibility are determined precisely in reference to the organizational exer- cise of social power.

To sharpen this change more, we might now respond to the question we left earlier: "What is the reasoning behind the pro- portionality principle?" The reasoning is rather simple:

(a)persons are the initiators of the exercise of power;
(b)power exercised in a society has effects on the values
   of persons in a society;
(c)given the Fundamental Ethical Principle, one who is
   responsible must use social power with conscious
   respect for the values of those affected.

Thus, the change in thought on social responsibility grows from a more accurate understanding of the TOTAL COST in the social system that accrues from the exercise of organizational power. Those who control such power, the managers, ethically stand accountable.

Kenneth R. Andrews compares the two expressions of social responsibilities in this way:[13]

Rather than wholly personal or idiosyncratic contributions (like supporting the museum one's wife is devoted to) or safe and sound contributions like the standard charities, or faddist entry into fashionable areas, corporate stra- tegic response to societal needs and expectations makes sense when it is closely related to the economic functions of the company or to the peculiar problems of the community in which it operates.
   For a paper company, it would seem a strategic necessity to give first priority to eliminating the poisonous efflu- ents from its mills rather than, for example, to support

cultural institutions like traveling art exhibits. Similarly, for an oil company it would seem a strategic necessity to look at its refinery stacks, at spillage, and at automobile exhaust.

The fortunate company that is paying the full social cost of its production function can make contributions to problems it does not cause.

The ethician judges that there is an ethical obligation of power wielders in respect to all the foreseeable effects of their actions. If the exercise of economic power has degraded the social or the physical environment, then there is ethical reason to judge that those in control of this power are bound to do what they can to "restore the harmony" in the social or the physical environment (fill out the total social cost).

This is the operative principle for managers to respond to social values beyond economic values in respect to what business does to society by its proper operations. If one could show that such activities as specific pollution controls were in fact effective means to restore such disrupted harmony, then one could argue for them.

Furthermore, the policy whereby the economic costs for the "restoration of harmony" are "passed on to the customers" is ethically unprincipled. It is necessary, according to managers. But it is "necessary" only if one is in a pure competiton situation with no profit margin to absorb the costs, or if one fails to use other than the pure economic horizon. For an oligopolistic corporation to pass such costs along to customers is to substitute the customers as the ones responsible for the disvalues at issue, and make them bear the rest of the total cost. This is ethically to deny responsibility for the exercise of power that caused the disharmonious effects in the first place.

In respect to that social responsibility involving what business could do for society, there is some argument that could be made that large corporational power also carries with it responsibility for adding to the general quality of life in a society. The argument is deductive. Those who are involved in a social system, either as individuals or as managers of institutional firms, benefit from the system, and therefore have a corresponding debt to contribute to the quality of the system. With the minor premise that business as an institutional group of firms both receives great benefits from the quality of life in the social system and is a potentially major instrument to influence that quality of life, the conclusion would appear to follow.

But there are two problems in the concretization of this responsibility of business to do for society, verification and tradeoffs.

There is need to verify, by utilitarian measure of consequences of alternate choices, the value of the programs suggested that business undertake (such as Affirmative Action hiring
and promotion), and a need to verify the validity of the expectations which insist on any such programs. The verification of
these expectations would base itself in a model of distributive
justice (studied in chapter four). Unfortunately, the verification of many programs suggested today for business more often
than not is omitted entirely or, worse, asserted in the face
of counterindicating facts.

Likewise, there is need to measure tradeoffs, whether these
are in economic costs or in political costs. Politically, the
tradeoff costs for business social action programs are enormous:
the growth of governmental influence, the rise in governmental
expenditures, the resultant increase in taxes and inflation, are
but the broad categories pertinent here. As these tradeoffs
become more serious, the verification of the value of the suggested programs which business is to do for society becomes the
more imperative.

CHAPTER   EIGHT

THE VIEW FROM THE MIDDLE

Within the individual corporation there are comples lines
of responsibility. Who is responsible, and how much anyone is
responsible for decisions, actions, and effects of the corporation seldom are immediately obvious. Such indefiniteness gives
the context for the success of the game of buck-passing.

Also, the theory of structuralism in sociology suggests
that organized human activities eventually take on a reality of
their own and individual human acts within such a sociological
unit respond to the logic of the "structure."

The person concerned with ethics in business may acknowledge that managers in corporations face this indefiniteness and
display this structuralistic response, but one cannot so acquiesce in this as to deny that individual human responsibility
also is a factor. The higher executive managers (and the middle managers to some extent) have both executive and judiciary
powers in corporations. They have power to control the corporation's actions to such an extent as to affect the income, the
property, and the manifold of other social values of several
groups of claimants. They make decisions that relate to the
corporation's contribution to the thrust of local, national, and
internation economy. They can act on behalf of the enterprise
against unions, other firms, governments, and societal units.

With such discretionary power, the manager must bring a
fine expertise to the role. And most managers today, when they
reflect on it, do base the legitimacy of their power on their
managerial skills. Some would even want the executives, or even
all managers, to receive the designation of "professional," to
indicate that it is "professed" special knowledge that merits
the position. Such a professional toning would rank the managerial expertise with other professions such as law, engineer-
ing, accounting, and medicine.

Peter Drucker suggests that busines managers, as members of
a leadership group in society, could fit the term "professional," and that this would base a special ethic of responsibility
for the manager.[1] He continues that the first responsibility
of the professional is "Above all, not knowingly to do harm,"
which is an exceptional possibility for the professional due to
the exclusively held knowledge used in decisions.

I suggest that the designation of "professional" could be
applied accurately to managers only if equivalents to the other

106

benchmarks of professions also appear in practice. These benchmarks are "dedication to service to social values by means of
the 'professed' special knowledge which is crucial for the society" (so that the general public could trust the ones who prac-
ticed the profession), and "clear, public norms of practice
within the profession with a review body within the profession
to sanction offenders."

The genesis of the call to rank managers as professionals
seems to be the development of the exclusively held expertise
demanded today in managers. This expertise fosters a sense of
independence in the manager, independence from that loyalty to
any given firm which marked the Organization Man in the past.
Granted that this independence is the mark also of a professional, still one must take note of the causes of the independence.
The professional is independent of loyalty to any particular
firm because the professional is committed in the use of the
professed expertise to definite values that are societal values
and which are higher than the values involved in any "position"
or any private firm. The skilled manager certainly has expertise that also is crucial for the social weal, at least in the
utilitarian "invisible hand" terms, but the independence in such
as the independent "gamesman" manager (as studied by Michael Maccoby) is based on the values in the challenge to use the expertise itself, and any societal values remain, for the manager,
ambiguous at best and functionless at worst. Thus, the "gamesman" manager is independent simply because one "could work for
anybody," and not because one has a committment to higher societal values.

To merit the appellation "professional," the manager would
have to have more than exclusive expertise and independence of
organizational loyalty. There would also have to be a social
goal functional in decisions and an intramural review board of
managers with sanction power for misuse of the social ranking.

Each professional keeps central to evaluation the thought,
"I am responsible." But how much is anyone responsible in a
corporation? To conclude that just the board of directors or
just the president and top executives are responsible is facile
but unrealistic. The ethical principle functions here: each
person who is in some managerial position, who is in some position to affect the making and the executing of company actions
or policies, is to some extent ethically responsible for such.

I. Ethical Problems and Middle Managers

Peter Drucker insists that the traditional definition of
the manager as "one who is responsible for the work of others"
emphasizes a secondary characteristic.[2] To identify persons who
are managers, the first characteristic is not command over peo-

ple, but responsibility for contributions. "Function rather than power has to be the distinctive criterion and the organizing principle."[3] (Obviously he writes here in reference to management theory. For ethics, function specifies the kind of power one has that is significant for ethical responsibility.) Drucker describes five basic operations in the work of the manager: "set objectives, organize, motivate and communicate, measure, and develop people."[4]

Middle managers especially have undergone a change in function. From those with downward authority, the new middle managers essentially are suppliers of knowledge, with responsibility, not authority, sideways.[5] Formerly, middle managers were expected (a)to translate general policies and broad plans into specific workable programs and systems; (b)to interpret management to subordinates; and (c)to interpret prevailing supervisory and employee needs, attitudes, and problems to upper management. Middle managers traditionally were the intersectors. From this function wherein one did not make but only carried out decisions, the middle manager today, as a knowledge supplier in such roles as manufacturing engineer, process specialist, tax accountant, market analyst, product and market manager, advertising and promotional specialist, has impact on decisions themselves.[6]

For the rest of this chapter I will concentrate on the middle manager insofar as such a person shares in the power and pressures of corporational organization. In many ways, the ethical immediacy is more obvious for the middle manager. The middle manager is more immediately aware of the cost of decisions in terms of intrafirm sweat and tears. Human beings and human values within the firm often are more apparent to one such.

To start, it will be useful to review some surveys which have tested out over the past fifteen years ethical sensitivity of managers to many problem areas.

(A)One of the early surveys that bore witness to the managerial ethical conflicts was done by Raymond Baumhart, S.J.[7] Baumhart's survey covered all levels of management. One of the results was a listing by the managers themselves of situations of business-ethics conflicts. They ranked these as follows:

(a)hiring and layoffs;
(b)honest communication;
(c)opportunities for collusion and other sharp practices in pricing;
(d)gifts, entertainment, and kickbacks;
(e)pressure from superiors.

The ranking has one interesting flaw. Baumhart's survey actual-

ly involved a rather high percentage of top managers. Later
surveys lead one to conclude that this high percentage may have
affected the ranking in a most crucial way. When these later
surveys limited their population to only middle managers, (e)
becomes dominant and the other four, (a), (b), (c), and (d) become channels for the middle managers' responses to (e).

(B) A second survey, directed by C. E. Evans of Wayne State
University, concentrated on middle managers.[8] The respondents
ranked the business-ethics conflicts as follows:

   (a) complying with superior's requirements when they con-
       flict with one's code of ethics;
   (b) job demands infringing on home obligations;
   (c) methods employed in competition for advancement;
   (d) avoiding or hedging responsibility;
   (e) maintaining integrity when it conflicts with being
       well-liked;
   (f) impartial treatment of subordinates because of race,
       religion, or personal prejudice;
   (g) moral concern that one's job does not fully utilize
       one's capacities;
   (h) condoning poor quality;
   (i) knowingly giving less-than-best performance;
   (j) misrepresentation of facts.

(C) A recent survey, conducted by Archie B. Carroll, once
again tested how managers themselves perceive the ethics-related
issues of business.[9] Professor Carroll states the objective of
the survey. "To determine the manager's views on (actually
printed) statements which postulated allegations concerning the
state of business ethics today and the relationship between
business morality and political morality, as exemplified by
Watergate." For us, three interpretations by the author concerning the result of the survey are of special importance.

   (a) About 78 percent of manager respondents agreed that the
       person "down the line" would at times compromise one's
       ethics to achieve results.

   (b) The reason one would probably so compromise ethics would
       be because of the pressures from the top to satisfy
       organizational expectations.

   (c) Yet the great majority of top managers deny that pres-
       sure so to compromise one's ethics exists today in
       business.

Apparently, writes Carroll, "top management can be inadvertently
insulated from organizational reality with respect to particular
issues."

II.   Three Ethical Pressures on Middle Managers

Before I take up these pressure sources, I must note two
factors which mitigate some of the ethical demands on middle
managers today. First, there is a real and often legitimate
ethical pluralism amidst the managers who make judgments on an
action or policy. Several managers might disagree honestly on
the ethical implications or even on the factual effects of actions or policies. When this happens on the same managerial
level within a company, the ethical demand from the problem forces some resolution of the conflict even as the indefeasible
conscience of each person is respected. (A suggestion: get all
to express what principles and values they see at issue.)   Second, whenever the complexities of implications grow, there grows
in importance with them the distinction between what is possible
and what is ideal. The ethician acknowledges the reasonable effort to foresee effects and the reasonable utilization of the
principle of the double effect. Even though some harm may, or
even certainly will accrue to human values as a result of a company's action or policy, if the result which is harmful can
qualify as a rational double effect, to decide to execute the
policy could still be ethically good. With these notations of
mitigating factors, I now take up three pressure sources on the
ethics of middle managers.

(A) Pressure from Business Superiors. For easier treatment, let
us distinguish three kinds of pressures from top management that
can be felt by middle managers: "produce or else";"act questionably"; and "do the right thing but also produce."

(A1) "Produce or else." Top management policy can complicate the ethical evaluation of middle managers by insisting on
a certain share of the market, by setting too large a sales
quota, by establishing too high a profit margin, and so on. It
is up to the middle manager to translate these demands into op-
erational procedures and the pressure is very great to grasp the
more expedient measures.

We must be precise on what is the source of the ethical
difficulty here. It is not in terms simply of the pressure to
produce as an efficient manager. This pressure in itself is
part of the "game," part of the "heat of the kitchen" of business. The source of the ethical difficulty is that this pressure shifts the responsibility for results to the middle manager, and yet those who apply the business pressure within an organization do not clarify the limits of the pressure. One is
called upon to gain a share of the market, a certain sales
quota, a certain profit margin. Unless it is clearly spelled
out and believed that, if a middle manager has a shortfall in
these areas and can explain it as necessary because of ethical
limitations on available methods, the top management, far from

criticism, will find a way to encourage such decisions within the organization itself, the only realistic attitude of the middle manager would be to act at times unethically to achieve the organization's economic objectives and to sacrifice, according to some societal value standard, objectives one should ethically support.

One must keep in mind that adequate communications upward, by which top management gains understanding of what its policies and goals imply in practice, are not to be presumed. Consequently, it is an ethical demand in itself that good communications be established even at the cost of initial discomfort. In our experience, pressure toward unethical practices eventually becomes irresistable and contravenes a person acting well.

(A2) "Act questionably." Sometimes top management directly pressures middle managers to act illegally or, if this is unclear, to act in ethically "gray areas." Kenneth R. Andrews comments: "If it's black and white, and a man has normal courage and security, he'll say no. It's in the gray area that a businessman may more likely founder."[10]

Probably the most common gray area in which pressure builds from the business-ethics tension for the middle manager is with the call from the top for the "controlled disclosure." As one edits reports, the manager feels pressure to omit significant facts or trends or even suspicions if the receiver of the report (within or without the company) would think more of the company or of the individual, or of the individual's boss, if the item is omitted or obfuscated. The revelations of such a practice in recent court cases and congressional investigations indicate how few escape this pressure.

(A3) "Do the right thing but also produce." Some top managers complicate the already convoluted problems of effectiveness-ethics by what amounts to corporate ambivalence, a "do the right thing but also produce" simultaneity. At least this has often been the content of the corporate message as heard by the middle managers. The electrical price-fixing collusion at the start of the 1960's was one example how the attitudes of top management were heard by middle managers. The pressure to produce simply does not contain adequate provision to allow for ethical actions in the real circumstances of the time, even if top management "wishes" ethical actions and recommends them overall. When general norms are not updated along with new policy directives, the middle manager is split in weighing how to apply both.

(B) Pressure from Family-Related Obligation. A second major source of pressure on middle managers is that which comes from obligations that pertain to one's family. For some time many

have admitted that the life style of managers calls for "corporate bigamy." The dedication demanded of the middle manager,
often when one is between the ages of 30-45, could bring about
deep conflicts in the home life. Or it may be that the manager
remains cooperative in questionable practices due to the sense
of family responsibility and the fear that non-cooperation would
endanger the job.

To the corporation, the manager is related by ties of justice from a contract and by the principle of expediency in terms
of job improvement. To the family, the manager is related by
love, respect for persons, concern for the future, and the like.
Up to now, the policy of corporations has generally ignored corporate middle managers' families, especially the wives. "Their
cruelty has been as much out of machismo as malice. The question they ask first is, How can the wife be of help to the company?...Until recently we have accepted facile explanations and
rationalizations of disintegrative behavior of spouses and children on the bases of inherent weakness or inferiority. Psychol-
ogy most conveniently supplied the rhetoric...to hide inordinate
stresses and injustices as a result of repeated uprooting in the
name of progress and opportunity."[11] We now understand better
the effects of this corporate subordination of the needs and
values of the spouses of middle managers. The continual moves
rob them of their identities and sense of self-worth because,
unlike the manager spouse, they are without the energy or the
opportunity to reestablish themselves in the new surroundings.

(C) <u>Pressure from Peers in Intrafirm Competition</u>. There are two
major areas of pressure from intrafirm competition that are
sources for tension as the middle manager tries to combine good
ethics and good business. The first is the game-maneuvers behind the scenes. The second is the hesitation to speak out when
faced with an ethical problem about using certain means for
business objectives. The former intends a less than advantageous appearance for an intrafirm rival, the latter avoids a
possibly bad appearance for oneself.

(C1)Many middle managers are convinced that a person cannot
move up in rank if one does nothing in peer competition except
actions which one considers honest and decent. (Top managers
hold the same conviction.[12]) And sometimes these other than
honest and decent methods receive subtle encouragement to pre-
pare upcoming top executives to function with "drive and aggres-
siveness," even though few would say this outloud today.

Some of the more familiar procedures that might be classified as other than honest and decent---such as idea stealing,
planting doubts about another, withholding facts to put one's
immediate superior in a poor light---are resorted to even by
regular abstainers when there is a time of business crisis (re-

cession, merger, restructuring).

One must take care to evaluate maneuvers within intrafirm competition. On the analogy of games, one may be frustrated if outmaneuvered, but one can hardly claim all suicide squeeze plays or long passes on third-and-one are unethical. Still, certain maneuvers are outside protection of the game horizon, (a)because the maneuver is directed not at another in terms of game play, but in terms of human player (for example, the competition eliminators such as "planting doubts about another," "knifing the absentee," and "withholding critical facts to put another in a bad light"); or (b)because the maneuver is unfair, that is, within the game situation there is not equal opportunity to defend or rebut.

(C2) Several years ago, Stuart Chase wrote an essay titled "The Luxury of Integrity." In it he wrote of the plight of the middle managers of corporations who do not have the security to speak out against the positions of higher managers. Some would argue that this plight is now alleviated and that initiative, creativity, moderately phrased corrections of those higher, and so on, are encouraged. Douglas McGregor influenced many people in this direction.[13] He distinguished and clarified two sets of assumptions about human motivation and argued that these two sets produced two theories, Theory X and Theory Y, about the problems of administration and organization. Against Theory X, which holds that people dislike work, must be coerced, and want to avoid responsibility, McGregor urged Theory Y, which involved an integration of corporational and middle manager goals by means of encouragement of initiative, self-direction, creativity, responsible suggestions, and the like. (Clarence Walton suggests that the popularity of McGregor's analysis is indicative of the two attitudes of Adams and Jefferson on human nature in our American psyche.[14]) More recently, John J. Morse and Jay W. Lorsch suggest a new set of assumptions and argue for a "Contingency Theory: the fit between task, organization and people."[15] They argue that the appropriate pattern of organization is contingent both on the nature of the work and on the particular needs of the people involved. They use as one central need in all human motivation "to achieve a sense of competence." Such a contingency theory finds decentralization and participation by middle managers in decisions, urged by McGregor, as neutral in the abstract. In the area of practical operations today, studies on the multinational corporations suggest these have usually a strict hierarchy in decision making.[16]

Even if a corporation operates with Theory Y so that "in theory" the middle manager could speak out of ethical hesitations, it would take only one top official per company to destroy the desires of many top managers, and it takes only the feeling among middle managers that there is pressure to be silent and compromise one's ethics to do the damage.

Recently psychologists have suggested that other factors might be at work also in the reluctance to speak out. Besides the risk of a setback in competitive standing, the middle managers might also suffer a classical syndrome of groups. When a person is within a social body the person often hesitates to act "until someone else does." There is a fear, at least cultural, of putting one's head on the block first. Insofar as this syndrome is operative, I do not think it can be ignored as a mitigating factor for ethical evaluation. However, as a lack of a virtue, courage, the hesitancy cannot be dismissed as simply a psychological factor which totally excuses, either.

A more likely rationalization for the reluctance to speak out on questionable practices will lead us to the next section. The organizational situatedness engenders a feeling of community and loyalty that becomes a bias in all judgments in favor of the organization. Experientially, such a bias fosters an efficient and satisfactory life-situation in the organization. And no organization could continue without it. But one must take care how the organizational situatedness affects the ethical evaluation by each person.

III. Cooperation and Probabilism

Because people need institutions, and because the business institution consists of such things as large corporations, one does not find it incredible that persons who work for a corporation can identify with its interests. One today terms this identification "conformity." In his book, The Organization Man, William H. Whyte, Jr., suggested, and later investigations have supported him, that business corporations are not unique atmospheres for conformity.[17] A certain degree of conformity must be in those who work within any organization or else nothing cooperative will occur. Ethically a problem arises only as such conformity cuts across other relationships: one's interests that are one's own and other than those of the corporation; the interes of those not in the corporation; and so on.

The matter is complicated further by the presence of a variety of conceptual models of corporational conformity which interpret the type of conformity expected. Since these affect ethical factors, I will review four such models here.[18]

1. "The machine model." In this model, success finds usual expression in terms of productivity and efficiency. All items, including employees, are looked on as if they were primarily cost elements. Everything is priced. Conformity is in terms of complete, unthinking functionality.

2. "The biological model." In this model, one views the corporation itself as a living organism, and so success is analogous to success as a living organism: preservation, health, and a maximization of "rational interests." Conformity is health, and lack of conformity means a problem that must be "treated" with a view primarily toward the health of the total organism.

3. "The intra-mural game model." In this model, which more often functions in larger, multiple-product firms, success is registered if there is "healthy competition" among employees and among departments. Rewards go to the "winning" person or to the "winning" team. One sees conformity as a call to help the team.

4. "The human subsystem model." In this model, one is hard pressed to uncover a simple description of either success or of conformity. There would have to be something in terms of the transmission and achievement of human values by members within the firm and by the firm as an organized subsystem of the whole social system. Conceptually, this model has two major difficulties: (a) it goes beyond commonly accepted models; and (b) it calls for judgment about values that are not readily quantifiable and which, consequently, are not all that clear.

Whatever the model by which conceptualized, the fact of conformity as an experienced secondary horizon is ethically supportable as a utilitarian need and as a social integration need. As mentioned, ethical problems arise as such conformity cuts into relationships that fall under other horizons, such as one's personal life, the lives of those outside the corporation, and so on.

With the spectrum of responsibility that functions within corporations, and with the variety of actions and policies which may ethically be questionable and even at the moment unresolvable, and with the fact of ethical pluralism and honest disagreement, there is need for some rules of thumb for the ethically serious person who works in today's corporation. As a contribution to these rules of thumb, I offer comments on the ethical tradition concerning cooperation in evil, probabilism in uncertain evaluations, and "whistle-blowing." I will treat the first two together, and take up whistle-blowing subsequently.

(A) Cooperation in Evil. Whenever an employee judges that a corporation's action or policy or practice is ethically wrong, that employee must also grow concerned over one's contribution to such actions or policies or practices as a member of the business organization. This concern witnesses to the matter that ethical tradition designates as "cooperation in evil." The matter about which concern exists is that one who cooperates in evil is at least a partial cause of the evil done. How partial a cause varies widely, and the ethical tradition suggests we

might see in this variety ethical as well as unethical cooperation. In order to clarify these two manners of cooperation, we
must first do more preparatory delineation of kinds of cooperation. "Cooperation in evil" may be defined as "any help afford-
ed to another in unethical behavior." From experience we discover many actions that fit this formal definition.

Specifically, (#1)one may command another to do the unethical action or to continue the unethical practice; (#2)one may
by words or action urge or advise another to the unethical action or practice; (#3)one may consent as one among many who vote
for the unethical action or practice; (#4)one may give encouragement that one knows will confirm another in the unethical action or practice; (#5)one may conceal or defend the unethical
action or practice; (#6)one may physically help in a facet of
the unethical action or practice; (#7)one may participate in the
beneficial results of the unethical action or practice; (#8)one
may contribute to the means, condition or atmosphere requisite
for the unethical action or practice; and (#9)one may fail to
act to prevent the unethical action or practice or the damage
by these to persons before, during, or after the fact.

Cooperation is called positive if the cooperation consists
in an overt act which is important to the unethical behavior.
Cooperation is called negative if the cooperation consists in
forbearance which does not impede the behavior or its issue.

The tradition tells us that cooperation in evil can be either ethical or unethical. There is yet one more division we
need to express clearly which is which. One can join in the
action or practice itself by actual performance, or one can join
in by supplying with the needed means with the intention of aid-
ing the performance. Such joining-in traditionally has been
called formal cooperation. One can also, by what one does as a
member of the organization, supply with the needed means, needed
conditions, or needed atmosphere, join in the action or practice, or one can join in simply with the refrain from interfer-
ence as one does one's own job. Traditionally such joining-in
has been called material cooperation.

The difference between formal and material cooperation
hinges on the intention: if one wants the evil or if one wants
the issue of the evil action or practice, the cooperation is
formal; if neither, the cooperation is material. Formal cooperation, as a decision for doing the unethical, is unethical.
Material cooperation may be ethical (justified) or unethical
(unjustified). The heart of the justification is the application of the principle of the double effect. For this principle
to function, of course, there would have to be a second issue
to the action or practice, which second issue is such a value
that it bases a sufficient reason for the cooperation. The val-

ue would base a sufficient reason only if it were proportional
to the evil involved and proportional to the degree of participation involved.

The rule of thumb for material cooperation is: "I can permit others to use my actions or noninterference as part of the
means or background context for unethical performances if a proportionately grave reason exists for me to continue to do what
I am doing." Again here the long term ramifications of any action I may take must be suitable as I keep in mind the difference in progressive living between the possible and the ideal.

(B) Probabilism. There are times when ethically we are not
sure. Yet some of these times require that we act, that we decide whether or not to act or to cooperate. The tradition concerning Probabilism speaks to these times.

If the investigation or the pressure of time leaves one
still in doubt on the moral adequacy of what is about to do, the
experience of persons indicates that the good conscience is satisfied by indirect certitude, that is, by the use of a reasonable procedure for the decision on the very doing of an action
as distinct from judgment on what one does in the action. Even
though the value of the content of the act is in no way more
disclosed by means of this rule of thumb of Probabilism, the
doubt concerning the placing of the act nevertheless is removed.

The tradition of Probabilism holds that, in cases of uncertainty as to the ethicality of any concrete action, if there
exists a "really probable opinion" for both alternatives, that
is, if one can make a case (strong or weak is not the point) for
the action as right and as wrong, then liberty exists and one
may ethically do either alternative. This openness to either
alternative remains even if a stronger case can be made for one
side. As long as there is honest uncertainty on the ethicality
of an action, it must be the case that there are good but not
conclusive reasons for both sides. These reasons may be because
of one's personal experience (called intrinsic probability) or
because of one's understanding of the reflection on experience
by others (called extrinsic probability). As long as there is
either intrinsic probability or extrinsic probability, there
exists the requisite "really probable opinion." Even if the
opposition opinion on the ethicality of the action is held to be
more probable, the ethical person may decide for either alternative. Without certainty, either opinion may be false, and the
less probable opinion may be the true one. This possibility is
at the heart of Probabilism, and seems incontrovertible.

The arguments for Probabilism are two. (1)An ethical precept only binds a person if that precept is clear and certain

about the envisaged action. An ethical precept cannot bind rationally or psychologically if the person understands that it is really probable that the action envisaged and its omission both are ethical. (This in the tradition is: lex dubia non obligat; non potest lex incerta certam obligationem inducere.) (2)The ethical judgment (conscience) of the thoughtful and free person is not coerced to a specific decision on an action unless the action manifestly and conclusively is seen to be the right one or the wrong one at this time.[19]

It is important to note that Probabilism insists that feeling is not conclusive in ethical decisions. One may feel that an action is wrong, and yet have probable reason to go ahead and do it and judge the doing of it to be ethically right.

Of course, there are preconditions for the use of this rule of thumb. First is the desire to do the right thing. Second is the balance between the risk taken (the amount of harm that may be done if the alternate act has the value) and the reasons why one must act and act with the indirectly certain conscience.

IV. Whistle Blowing

From both legal justice and ethical justice, the employee owes loyalty, obedience and confidentiality to the corporation. Yet with the recent sensitivity toward the public effects of actions of corporations, there has come reflection on the meaning of loyalty, obedience, and confidentiality.[20] Some have viewed any change with suspicion. Mr. James M. Roche, former chairman of the board of General Motors, attacks as follows:

> Some of the enemies of business now encourage an employee
> to be disloyal to the enterprise. They want to create sus-
> picion and disharmony, and pry into the proprietary inter-
> ests of the business. However this is labelled---indus-
> trial espionage, whistle blowing, or professional respon-
> sibility---it is another tactic for spreading disunity
> and creating conflict.[21]

This is a perfect example of the use of the economic horizon solely to interpret human events. Whether or not the particular proponents of whistle blowing that Mr. Roche has in mind really have the evil intent Mr. Roche suspects, the point is that Mr. Roche does not appear able to consider that the actions could be interpreted in another manner under another horizon. Mr. Phillip I. Blumberg finds a different common core in recent developments than does Mr. Roche: "the right of the employee of the large public corporation to take action adverse to the interests of his employer in response to the employee's view as to the proper social responsibility of his corporate employer."[22]

The catch-name for this today is "whistle blowing." It may be described as the action taken by anyone who on one's own judgment draws a line where the ethical values involved force one to transcend loyalty to one's business corporation and to expose publicly what one considers the unconscionable practices of one's own business.[23] Ethically, three factors seem important in principle for whistle blowing.

(1) The employee's duty to the corporation in terms of loyalty, obedience, and confidentiality.

(2) The employee's right to a reasonable hierarchy of values in ethical judgment in times of conflicts of rights.

(3) The society's rights in terms of the effects of actions by the corporation, especially with respect to the need by the members of society to have those who know alert the society to the dangers of what is being done in our complex organizational and technological world.

Corporate managers are among the first to know and are among the few able to evaluate with any degree of expertise such items as the following:[24]

a) defective vehicles in the process of being marketed to unknowledgeable customers;
b) industrial dumping of possibly dangerous waste;
c) large waste of government funds by private contractors;
d) patterns of discrimination;
e) willful deception in advertising;
f) lack of proper testing of a product;
g) suppression of negative results of testing;
h) suppression of serious occupational disease data.

The middle manager owes loyalty, obedience, and confidentiality to the corporation. With recent thought, these three duties have undergone some modification. Kenneth D. Walters sums up part of the new attitude:[25]

The basic assumption...is that employees who disagree with organizational policies on grounds of conscience are obliged not to quit their jobs but to remain in their organizations and act as forces for change from within.

This is a new concept of loyalty in business. And whistle blowing also involves new ethical attitudes toward obedience and confidentiality. There is consideration of "legitimate dissent" and "legitimate going public." The courts have given some legal guidelines which stress the importance of the motive to serve the public good to make dissent legitimate, and the importance of the right of free expression in legitimate breach of confi-

dentiality. Walters cautions that so far these court guidelines have come only in respect to whistle blowers in government
and public organizations. But he cites two legal scholars who
predict the expansion in the future into private organizations.

> A system of freedom of expression that allowed private
> bureaucracies to throttle all internal discussion of their
> affairs would be seriously deficient. There seems to be
> general agreement that at some points the government must
> step in.[26]

> (Whistle blowing) will become an area of dynamic change in
> the corporate organization and in time will produce signif-
> icant change in established legal concepts.[27]

In our day, the imperative toward whistle blowing comes not
only from the general ethical parameter on cooperation in the
unethical actions and practices, but also, now that technology
and manufacturing procedures have become so complex, from the
fact that customers do not have the ability to judge quality or
effects of corporational acts and products as they once did. So
those who work in the corporation, those who have some expertise
and some knowledge, are often the only ones who can speak out
for the rights and interests of those in society. This willy-
nilly sets a greater ethical burden on middle managers than was
true in the past. The rule of thumb here is: "Ethical obligation is proportional to exclusivity and potentiality held by
corporations to affect societal values." Because we have not
had too much time as yet to reflect on the sound discernment
that should precede whistle blowing, a few suggestions ethically
are in order.[28]

1. Is my knowledge of the situation reasonably comprehensive
   and accurate?
2. Just exactly what are the objectionable matters, and what
   public values are endangered?
3. Why is the company doing such objectionable actions? For
   example, the suppression of negative test results may or
   may not have a legitimizing "double effect."
4. How substantial do I foresee to be the unfair harm to others?
   How irreversible the harm? Will there be offsetting gains?
5. How far should I go and can I go inside the organization with
   my concern or objection?
6. Would it be better to keep silent on this issue and work
   within the corporation to attempt to curtail such practices
   in the future? How do I decide this?
7. Is the excuse, if we did not do it, somebody else (a competitor)would, really good enough?

CHAPTER   NINE

ADVERTISING

In essence, advertising has two tasks: to call the attention of the receiver to something, and to persuade the receiver
toward something. Both these tasks are, generically, modes of
communication and one would do well to approach the ethics of
advertising with this in mind. But more specifically, one
should attend to the intention "to persuade" in the tasks of
advertising, and I will concentrate on this.

Nothing that is so easy to humans could be a total danger.
And all humans are easily susceptible to persuasion. All persons accept agreeable courses of action and attitudes from others. Indeed, they must, for they are incapable of thinking
through all the actions required in daily living. Persons are
susceptible to persuasion, usually without paying too much attention to the reasonableness of the action or the attitude,
out of a need for survival.

Still, persuasion has never been taken lightly by the ethician. Plato argued against the Sophists that, if persuasion
were the only, or were the supreme species of human communication, then all human communication would be undermined. Persuasion is communication which has as its goal, not the communication of what is the case, but the persuasion that such and
such is the case, whether it is the case or not. As a result,
the public zone of trust which is necessary for human communication, the presumption of credibility that others will tell one
what is the case, deteriorates. And this public zone of trust
is a mediated right of all human persons. It is derivative
from, or mediated by, the primary to true information which information is needed to act well as thoughtful and free persons.
The right to the zone of trust is a derivative right as the
necessary condition for credible communication, the condition
without which no hearer or seeker of truth could have assurance
that truth was to be expected in communication. Ethicians have
always thought that those who use persuasion bear the onus of
proof that its employment is not deleterious to the public zone
of trust in communications between persons.

I. The Benefit Side of Advertising

Using the postulate of economics that the human person has
insatiable appetites and primary self-interest, and using a general reference to the media employed, one can define advertising

121

formally as "the use of intermediate means to persuade a potential customer why it is in the customer's best interest to buy the goods one has for sale."

Because of the natural restrictions on knowledge in the human condition, what this vacuous and formal description identifies is on the surface neither dishonest nor dehumanizing. On the contrary, the procedure has brought about benefits both to the businessperson and to the consumer.

On the side of business.

1. Advertising is necessary because of time: (a)as goods are produced to be exchanged, it is good that they should be exchanged as quickly as possible; (b)as every producer is occupied in producing what others want, it is good that the producer should always be able to find without delay and without uncertainty, others who want the products.[1]

2. Advertising is necessary because of the proliferation of products of the same quality, at least with respect to the consumer's ability to judge. Name brand identification makes the producer's product stand out.

3. Advertising promotes consumer spending which opens to firm expansion, economies of scale, and more employment.

On the side of the consumer.

1. We have evidence that familiarity by means of brand name is itself important for consumers. Even if told that two products are qualitatively the same, people will prefer known brand named products, even if such are higher priced. Apparently, familiarity is a value. William James first studied the feeling of "being at home with something" and titled such the "sentiment of rationality."

2. As long as this "at-homeness" is maintained, the consumer also can find value in experimentation, value in newness itself, and the call to this newness will be heeded if it comes from a familiar source.

3. Advertising offers aesthetic value as well as an identification value. As it creates an image in reference to a product, advertising offers an improvement in the consumer's mind. (One here notes that all "no-identity" testing is not a test of the full value one gets from an aesthetically charged product.)

Consequently, in any ethical evaluation of advertising, one must bring in and acknowledge what presupposed values, in addition to the above one uses. Donald L. Kanter lists some general areas:[2]

    a)a vision of society in terms of its goals, its values,
       its beliefs, and its future;
    b)a conception of human nature and its vulnerability;
    c)an empirical assessment of advertising effectiveness;
    d)an attitude toward regulation and regulators.

(a)On the vision of society we might ask: "just how commercial
should any society be?" To measure the ethics of advertising in
terms of its contribution to people becoming more commercialis-
tic, one presupposes some standard on the limits that ought to
be on such an attitude. But how does one ascertain the limits?

(b)On the vulnerability of consumers, we might wonder how sim-
plified a conception of a "defenseless consumer" is. Evidence
seems to indicate a large capacity in people to weigh advertising in light of actual experience, experience that is either
with or of the product advertised.

(c)On the empirical assessment of advertising's effectiveness,
many experts suggest that we do not as yet have universally acceptable ways to measure this. Those who argue that advertising
is the cause of false wants, poor taste in selections, and so
on, imply more than can be verified. This is not to say that
ethically one must not issue a caveat on the basis of the in-
complete correlations already at hand. One must act with what
one has. But one must keep a distinction in mind here. There
is no empirical basis as yet for any general proposition on the
effectiveness of advertising. Therefore, we cannot premise that
advertising "creates false values or false needs." But there is
evidence in certain particular areas that changes in consumer
behavior correlate with advertising campaigns. For example,
there is some evidence that the advertising of pharmaceutical
drugs on TV "may be reducing cognitive dissonance (personal conflicts) by implying, symbolically, to the users, that 'Everyone
turns on in his own way.' This might be an important rationalization for the furtive user."[3]

(d)On the attitude toward regulation and regulators, I only men-
tion it for completeness, as it refers to an area that is not
specific to advertising. It refers to the area of the legal
enforcement of standards and paternalism.

    Because of its potential for harm as well as for benefit,
I intend to scrutinize the practice of advertising as one type
of persuasion. I will look at ethical questions on its economic
presuppositions, a debate on its intended effect, its product
embellishment, and the means used in advertising.

II. A Presupposition and a Debate on Effect

John Kenneth Galbraith once noted that the "theory of consumer demand" is based on two broad propositions. One of these was "that wants originate in the personality of the consumer" and are merely part of what is given for the economic question.[4] The economist needs this proposition to support the thesis that each individual's insatiable wants are original in the person and are not contrived for the person, "and above all they must not be contrived by the process of production by which they are satisfied."[5]

The theoretical link between the wants, which the goods produced are presumed to satisfy, and the production of those goods itself comes from the societal value in the ability of the business institution to give us a high standard of living. This emphasis on the ability of the business institution to deliver the goods generates, as well as presupposes, a value in the acquisition and use of such "ever superior" goods and services. As the superior good or service is available, it is by definition valuable and consequently its acquisition and use are the object of an imperative.

The practical link between wants and the process of production, of course, is advertising. Galbraith terms advertising the enterprise of "modern want creation."[6] And he adroitly notes, "The fact that wants can be synthesized by advertising, catalyzed by salesmanship, and shaped by the discreet manipulations of the persuaders shows that they are not very urgent."[7]

In a well-to-do community we cannot be much concerned over what people are persuaded to buy. The marginal utility of money is low; were it otherwise people would not be open to persuasion.[8]

One must be careful here not to lose the point. People can be persuaded, Galbraith argues, only when their real wants are satisfied. One need not advertise water to one who thirsts, nor meat to one who is hungry. When the real needs ("those needs which are absolute in the sense that we feel them whatever the situation of our fellow human beings may be"---Keynes) are satisfied, then we are open to persuasion. Persuasion can then create wants in a psychological dimension beyond "real" needs.

But what is presupposed in this creation? (It is, of course, an empirical question whether advertisers do persuade effectively. This empirically is substantiated in only a few particular cases. Since we are concerned with the ethics for the practice, the ratio of activity to success is not immediately germane.) Presupposed must be that persons are open to be so persuaded toward the specification of additional wants! If persons did not have this amorphous tendency, then advertisers could not hope for success in their efforts to define and specify particular wants in addition to "real" or "absolute" wants.

How then are we ethically to evaluate such efforts to define and specify particular wants? Galbraith fears wants created by advertisers, because he sees this production of new wants as part of a syndrome (production, advertising, consumption) that must spiral to self-destruction. He calls this the "dependence effect." The condemnation of such a syndrome presupposes that it must continue of its own inner logic beyond the capacity of persons to moderate its effects. This syndromatic remorselessness would have to be proved. Furthermore, the hidden presupposition that any advertising that is not "constructive" (i.e., which does not supply the consumer straight information or some other useful service) gives no significant service and disregards the original needs and wants of consumers simply begs the ethical question. Apriori there is no reason to disregard the possibility that some human wants of significance are specified precisely by peer example and other social publicity, such as advertising. Perhaps without such examples and publicity certain original needs and wants would remain frustratingly unspecific.

Along these lines, F. A. Hayek has debated Galbraith on the conclusion that, if a consumer would not experience a desire or a want independently of advertising, that desire or want must be unreal, illusory, or unimportant.[9] To assert that a desire is not important because it is a learned element in the congeries of rising expectations would suggest that the whole cultural achievement of civil society is not important. In his attack, Hayek rightly debates that the basic presupposition behind Galbraith's "dependence effect" position is a principle even Galbraith would not wish to apply universally. Thus one errs to meatcleaver the set of desires into only two subsets: "real needs" and "needs which are simply dependent on the awareness that certain goods are in fact available."

The weakness of such a meatcleaver approach to desires would become apparent, writes Hayek, if one would apply its principle for the evaluation of desires to the areas of music, painting, and literature. There are no "independently determined desires" for Shakespeare's _Hamlet_. Certainly there were none before Shakespeare wrote it. Those in liberal education hope to create civilizing wants and desires in the students who educate themselves in its atmosphere. Thus, it is invalid apriori to consider sacrosanct the tastes and decisions of consumers before advertising enters, and to consider the resultant demands after advertising "artificial," and by artificial to connote "bad."

To assert simply that ads create needs is too vague, for the assertion without warrant reduces a complex result to one cause, the activities of the advertisers, and that one cause does not explain why ad persuasion succeeds. Galbraith has suggested as a second cause the diminishing marginal utility of money. That still gives no full explanation. To extrapolate from his own example, just as one does not have to persuade the thirsty person to want water, we know that one does not have to persuade people to be persuaded by ads. Until one offers an explanation for that, all talk of creation of needs, false or otherwise, or of manipulation of needs by advertisers remains deduction from unexamined premises.

People lack specificity in important human areas and ads offer items by which humans can identify some of their important wants. If this were not so, advertisers could not persuade anyone of anything. That any advertiser persuades by any ad indicates the real but as yet unspecified want which is there beforehand.

From this debate, we conclude that the ethics of advertising cannot be settled by simple appeal to the creation of wants. A more promising approach seems to be in terms of the wants specified by the advertisers and the intention of the advertisers in the persuasion. I am unsure about the authenticity of the wants specified by advertisers for I do not have any idiosyncratic theory by which to divide true specific wants from false specific wants. Only with an idiosyncratic theory could one talk of true and false wants, and such a theory would have to ignore the presence of the real unspecified wants that are the conditions for any persuasion and the absence of real specified wants which would prohibit any successful persuasion. The only procedure I have is empirically to look to ads and reflect on what nonspecific wants they presuppose and how they specify these nonspecific wants. These two steps direct the next two sections.

III.   The Product and the Embellishment

Ronald Gross writes succinctly, "Ads add." Ads add because the advertisers must say something about their products when there seldom is a significant difference between competing products.[10] Consequently, advertisers turn for the subject of their advertisements to the psychological needs of the consumer. "What ads add is us." Advertisers embellish their copy to externalize ways consumers can overcome felt inadequacies and change their situation from the way it is to the way it ought to be. The embellished product gives the consumers the identification of those items each needs to feel adequate. I find four main areas wherein people in our society feel inadequate.

(a)One may feel inadequate in a role, such as husband,
wife, father, mother. This expresses itself as a fear that one
does not perform as one ought and could if one was just not as
ignorant of what is needed by others and available. (b)One may
feel inadequate sexually and one needs that by which one can
feel in control in situations in which one has basic sexual insecurity. (c)One may feel inadequate socially and one needs
that by which one can feel in control in situations in which
one has basic social insecurity. Finally, (d)one may feel one
is inadequate so as unnecessarily "to miss out" on life's possible excitements because of life's contingencies.

The advertisers embellish their products and give the products "meaning" in reference to these four areas. By such embellishment, the advertisers gain some control in the market.

In a purely competitive market, which of course has never
existed in fact, the consumer is king. This consumer sovereign-
ty means two things: by virtue of demand, the consumer determines the allocation of resources; and the consumer enjoys goods
that are sold as cheaply and produced as abundantly as possible.
But in today's market, producers have more control. They employ
strategies, including the strategy of advertising, to influence
the market. With the rise of oligopolistic corporations and advertising, few seriously hold any more that the consumer's demands are in primary control of the market. That producers by
and large can and do create the demands for their products is
now assumed (even if not empirically established) as the matter
for ethical questioning.

The economic myth says that, if a product can be produced
and marketed profitably, then those in a free market have a
right to act accordingly. The ethician finds several acceptable
aspects in this mythology and a few questionable ones. No doubt
the businessperson must evaluate under the business horizon the
projected product in terms of questions such as: "Can we make
it?" "Can we make it sell?" and "Can we make it sell at an acceptable profit?" But inasmuch as all those involved and all
those affected by such an operation in the business enterprise
are human beings, the secondary horizon of business always has
its ethical justification from the criteria for legitimacy of
the business enterprise itself: the adequacy of the enterprise
to fill those needs which society has deemed legitimate.

No product would sell at all if some fragment of its potential was not connected with human needs. But is there any limit
in a technologically industrial economy to what degree one accepts in a product specification of needs and wants? This question ethically will not go away. If the businessperson does not
resolve the question, then the businessperson accepts the possibility of considering the consumer sheerly as a means for

profit and ignores the fact and the extent of effects by the
enterprise on the consumer's prima facie rights as a self-ordering person.

The entire problem takes on a new perspective, of course,
if the embellishment and distortion of advertising themselves
enhance positive human values. And this thesis is part of the
position forwarded by Theodore Levitt. He admits that today
the consumer is an amateur in the market, or even an "impotent
midget," and certainly not a king or queen. But he puts forward
the following:[11]

> Embellishment and distortion are among advertising's legit-
> imate and socially desirable purposes; and that illegit-
> imacy in advertising consists only of falsification with
> larcenous intent.

Levitt investigates both within the secondary horizon of advertising itself and also how this horizon relates to the general
ethical horizon. And quite amazingly, he claims that it is not
simply as persuasion but also as embellishment that advertising
has a human social value. For humans need to be shown hope in
material ways. He quotes Charles Revson of Revlon, Inc., "In
the factory we make cosmetics; in the store we sell hope."

To elaborate the function of embellishment for human life,
Levitt refers to the artistic decorations on Greek water jars.
The simple function to carry liquid did not explain why the pot-
ter decorated the jar. From this Levitt generalizes that the
literal functionality of the object does not exhaust the relationship of value that the human takes up toward the advertised
object. This relationship of value cannot be expressed by literal description alone (nor tested in "non-identity" "scientif-
ic" tests). Indeed, the symbolic substitutes with which humans
embellish their functional items are necessary to express, con-
ceptualize, and communicate the needed richness in life. Human
beings desire to embellish their lives and the advertiser, argues Levitt, supports this desire by the embellishment of economic products.

> Where have we arrived? Only at some common characteristics
> of art and advertising. Both are rhetorical, and both lit-
> erally false; both expound an emotional reality deeper than
> the "real"; both pretend to "higher" purposes, although
> different ones; and the excellence of each is judged by its
> effects on its audience---its persuasiveness in short. I
> do not mean to imply that the two are fundamentally the
> same, but rather that they both represent a pervasive, and
> I believe, universal, characteristic of human nature---the
> human audience demands symbolic interpretation in every-
> thing it sees and knows.[12]

The justification of this embellishment therefore rests on the value humans have in surpassing a life of insipid functionalism. If we add that, in our society, there is a reasonable expectation in the use of a secondary horizon such as advertising that the normal audience is sophisticated enough to be able to interpret the use of such a secondary horizon in matters such as embellishment (and indeed, we have evidence that such sophistication is quite the case, even among "culturally deprived" groups), we might conclude that embellishment as part of the art of persuasion used in advertising is serving a human value.

The general structure of this defense is that the consumer consumes in response to a problem faced in human living. The purpose of the purchase of a product is to solve a human problem. Advertising serves a useful and legitimate role insofar as it connects the product with the promise of such a problem resolution.

> Whether we are aware of it or not, we in effect expect and demand that advertising create these symbols for us to show us what life might be, to bring the possibilities that we cannot see before our eyes and screen out the stark reality in which we must live.[13]

One recalls here a basic presupposition of this defense: that, once the absolute needs of humans are satisfied, there is a further absolute need---to have specified and materialized before us ways whereby our lives can be fuller, more significant.

The unresolved ethical question focuses on the limits of such embellishments by advertising. Given that embellishments go beyond the literal functionality of an item, they would seem to be limited rationally in this way: they are to elicit only those hopes which the embellished product can in some way fulfill. Here an empirical test could suffice: repeated sales.

IV. The Means Used in Advertising

A. The arrest. The first step in the means of advertising is the procedure to arrest attention from the audience. With so many ads, and so many similar products, the potential customer must be grabbed. Among the devices used are those that might be classified under the rubrics of Beauty, Banging, and Brains. To get a potential customer's attention, the ad could employ something that strikes the senses as attractive (in all the ways which persons judge things as beautiful or appealing). Or the ad could employ an excessive sense stimulus that subtly alarms the receiver's expectancy (such as high noise, grating repetition, the dramatization of cultivated inanity). Or the ad could employ intellectual cleverness (humor, parody, original music).

B. The appeal. The second step in the means of advertising is the appeal to the consumer to respond to the product.
The effort here is to tie in one's product with some need, desire, or value in the potential customer. There are two manners of tying-in, often used concurrently. The one is the open
confrontation between a known need and a functional product.
The other is any mode of connection of the product with some
attitude, need, or desire not functionally conjoined with the
product. We will look at this below.

C. The mnemonic. The third step in the means of advertising is the bit out of the ad that the advertiser hopes will
stick in the consciousness of the potential customer. It need
not be, and usually is not, a direct aspect of the product's
functionality. More commonly, it is a catchly line, phrase,
tune, or dramatized inanity.

Let us concentrate on the appeal. Are there limits to what
means can be used to tie in a product with some attitude, need,
or desire not functionally conjoined with the product?

We have already encountered the position that advertising
contributes to the social reality of a product by adding embellishment to the functionality. And I have indicated four major
thematics that advertising has employed to specify and to mater-
ialize needs of humans beyond the absolute need level (the need
to feel role adequate, to feel sexually adequate; to feel socially adequate; and to feel that one does not unnecessarily
miss out in life's excitement), and to connect a given product
with the hope of the satisfaction of such needs. Consumers in
buying products do not buy simple functionals, they buy also
satisfaction through symbols. Thus, they do not buy cosmetics,
but the promise of beauty; not cigarettes, but social poise and
oral gratification; not a car, but a sense of male potency in
speed and performance.

The softpedalling of the consumer's reason by arousing emotions and sub-conscious tie-ins risks a dangerous passivity on
the side of the consumer, which passivity entails the reduction
of one's self-ordering of decisions. But this may be an acceptable "double effect" given the embellishment value.

The provoking of anxieties (such as in hawking the deficiency products: drugs, dentifrices, deodorents, detergents,
dandruff removers) can easily exceed the persuasion to buy a
product on the basis of embellishment and function. Certain
anxieties balloon out of proportion so easily that the hyper-
sensitivity to such areas of tension imbalances the sense of
sophisticated judgment.

The lowering of the sensitivity to human dignity can be

intended unethically in the arrest and mnemonic aspects, as well
as in the appeal. Examples here are "irritation" advertising
and "humiliation in role" advertising.

The deterioration of language is not a small issue according to which to evaluate advertising. Language itself is an
essential means in social existence. Language functions as an
instrument between persons as they communicate and respond, and
it functions in one's own private thinking and in one's own per-
ception and understanding of experience. The quality and the
nuance of thinking is a function of the quality of language at
one's command. Since contact and use affect the quality of
one's command of language, the terse, impact phraseology of advertising contributes to the reliance upon the immediately
available cliche. As George Orwell warns, the cliche suffers
from two ills: staleness of imagery and lack of precision. So
one can neither affix for oneself a meaning by a cliche, nor
assist another to reach a meaning through dialogue. And by a
vocal Gresham's Law, one who uses imprecise impact cliches finds
one's ability to call forth discriminative words and phrases, by
which to think and to assert independently, sink into desuetude.
Thus, the ability to self-order is affected directly by a deterioration of language. Orwell called for a consideration of
language, not in its literary use, "but merely language as an
instrument for expressing and not for concealing thought."14

Generally, that use of rhetoric we call advertising is
judged an acceptable instrument if it is in proportion to the
sophistication of the audience, and if it observes some limits
in addition to the "intrinsic principles of effectiveness."
Any use that has a denigration of human dignity is suspect.
Also, many potential responders might be harmed over a long
term of mass advertising because of the effects in the "atmosphere of thought and truth-telling." And deterioration of the
quality of language, finally, could only be risked through a
most exacting application of the principle of the double effect.

FOOTNOTES

NOTES FOR INTRODUCTION

1. Peter Drucker, Management (New York: Harper and Row, 1973), p. 366.
2. Peter Drucker, Management, pp. 368-375.
3. R. H. Tawney, Religion and the Rise of Capitalism (New York: New American Library, Mentor edition, 1947), p. 156.

NOTES FOR CHAPTER ONE

1. See Francis X. Sutton et al., The American Business Creed (New York: Schocken Books, 1962), p. 277.
2. Max Weber, The Protestant Ethic and the Spirit of Capitalism (New York: Charles Scribner's Sons, 1958), p. 159. See also Richard Eells and Clarence Walton, Conceptual Foundations of Business, 3rd ed. (Homewood, Ill: Irwin, 1974), pp. 342-345; Kenneth E. Boulding, "Religious Foundations of Economic Progress," Harvard Business Review, vol. 30 #3(1952), pp. 33-40.
3. Max Weber, The Protestant Ethic..., pp. 56-57.
4. Adam Smith, The Wealth of Nations, ed. Edwin Cannon (New York: The Modern Library, 1937), p. 423. In our time, see F. A. Hayek, "The Principles of a Liberal Social Order," in Studies in Philosophy, Politics and Economics (Chicago: The University of Chicago Press, 1967), esp. p. 163.
5. F. A. Hayek reports that the first ethical analysis of free exchange in an open market was done by Jesuit moralists in the 16th and 17th centuries. Law, Legislation and Liberty, vol. 2 (Chicago: The University of Chicago Press, 1976), note 15, pp. 178-179.
6. F. A. Hayek, Law, Legislation and Liberty, vol. 2, p. 110.
7. For criticism, see Irving Kristol, "When virtue loses all her loveliness---some reflections on capitalism and 'the free society'," in Daniel Bell and Irving Kristol, Capitalism Today (New York: New American Library, 1971), p. 21.
8. See F. A. Hayek, Studies in Philosophy,..., pp. 111,161.
9. Alfred D. Chandler, Jr., The Visible Hand: The Managerial Revolution in American Business (Cambridge: Belknap Press,1977).
10. Richard M. Huber, The American Idea of Success (New York: McGraw-Hill, 1971).

NOTES FOR CHAPTER THREE

1. Robert Warshow, "The Gangster as Tragic Hero," in The

Immediate Experience (New York: Doubleday, 1962), p. 132.

2. Warshow, "The Gangster...," p. 133.

3. Dale Tarnowieski, The Changing Success Ethic (New York: American Management Association, 1973), p. 17.

4. Richard M. Huber, The American Idea of Success (New York: McGraw Hill, 1971).

5. See also Harold L. Johnson, Business in Contemporary Society: Framework and Issues (Belmont, Calif: Wadsworth, 1971), pp. 59-60.

6. See John Rawls, "Two Concepts of Rules," Philosophical Review, 64(1955), pp. 3-32.

7. John Rawls, A Theory of Justice (Cambridge: Belknap Press, 1971), p. 55.

8. Rawls, A Theory..., p. 55.

9. See Richard Eells and Clarence Walton, Conceptual Foundations of Business, 3rd ed.(Homewood, Ill: Irwin, 1974), pp. 154-163.

10. Henry C. Wallich, The Cost of Freedom (New York: Harper & Bros., 1960), p. x.

11. Peter Drucker, Management (New York: Harper and Row, 1973), pp. 59-61.

12. Peter Drucker, Management, p. 61

13. Campbell R. McConnell, Economics, 6th ed.(New York: Mc-Graw-Hill, 1975), p. 635.

14. Peter Drucker, Management, pp. 369-372.

15. Rawls, A Theory..., p. 75.

NOTES FOR CHAPTER FOUR

1. Robert Nozick, Anarchy, State,and Utopia (New York: Basic, 1974).

2. See Hugo A. Bedau, "Egalitarianism and the Idea of Equality," in J. Roland Pennock and John W. Chapman, Nomos IX: Equality (New York: Atherton, 1967), pp. 3-27.

3. See Edward and Onora Nell, "On Justice under Socialism," Dissent (Summer, 1972).

4. David Hume, An Enquiry Concerning the Principles of Morals, Sect. III, part ii.

5. See F. A. Hayek, "The Principles of a Liberal Social Order," in Studies in Philosophy, Politics and Economics (Chicago: The University of Chicago Press, 1967), pp. 166-172.

6. See John Rawls, A Theory of Justice (Cambridge: Belknap Press, 1971), p. 305.

7. See John Rawls, "Constitutional Liberty and the Concept of Justice," Nomos VI: Justice (New York: Atherton, 1963), pp. 102, 118. Also, F. A Hayek, Law, Legislation and Liberty, vol. 2 (Chicago: The University of Chicago Press, 1976), chapter 9.

NOTES FOR CHAPTER FIVE

1. See Kenneth E. Boulding, Principles of Economic Policy (Englewood Cliffs, N.J.: Prentice-Hall, 1958), ch. 4; Harold L. Johnson, Business in Contemporary Society: Framework and Issues (Belmont, Calif: Wadsworth, 1971), pp. 11-12.

2. Robert L. Heilbroner and Lester C. Thurow, The Economic Problem, 4th ed. (Englewood Cliffs, N.J.: Prentice-Hall,1975), p. 157.

3. See F. A. Hayek, The Road to Serfdom (Chicago: The University of Chicago Press, 1944), Phoenix Books, p. 36.

4. F. A. Hayek, Studies in Philosophy, Politics, and Economics (Chicago: The University of Chicago Press, 1967), pp. 166-173.

5. F. A. Hayek, The Road to Serfdom, p. 101.

6. F. A. Hayek, The Road to Serfdom, pp. 101-102.

7. See Christopher Jencks et al., Inequality: A Reassessment of the Effects of Family and Schooling in America (New York: Basic Books, 1972), p. 3.

8. See John Rawls, A Theory of Justice (Cambridge: The Belknap Press, 1971), pp. 522-523.

9. Heilbroner and Thurow, The Economic Problem, pp. 173-174.

10. Joseph Schumpeter, Theory of Economic Development (Cambridge: Harvard University Press, 1934); Peter Drucker, Management (New York: Harper and Row, 1973), pp. 72-73.

11. Bernard W. Dempsey, S.J., The Functional Economy (Englewood Cliffs, N.J.:Prentice-Hall,1958), pp. 337-344.

12. Alfred D. Chandler, Jr., The Visible Hand: The Managerial Revolution in American Business (Cambridge: The Belknap Press, 1977), pp. 1, 484.

13. See Kenneth E. Boulding, "Economics as a Moral Science," American Economic Review, vol. 78, #2(1969), pp. 1ff.

14. Cited in Leon Hickman, "Prices, Competition and Morality," in The Ethics of Business, edited by Courtney Brown (New York: Columbia Graduate School of Business, 1963), pp. 16-35. Reprinted in Walton and Eells, The Business System (New York: Macmillan, 1967), pp. 569-581. Cited from The Business System, p. 573.

15. Leon Hickman, "Prices...," pp. 575-580.

16. Peter Drucker, Management, p. 58.

17. Frank Hyneman Knight, "The Ethics of Competition," first published in Quarterly Journal of Economics, vol. 37(1923), pp. 579-624. Reprinted in The Ethics of Competition (New York: Harper and Bros., 1935), pp. 41-75. All citations are from this reprint. See also, Eugene V. Rostow, "The Ethics of Competition Revisited," California Management Review, vol. 5 #3(1963).

18. Knight, The Ethics of Competition, p. 45.

19. Knight, The Ethics of Competition, p. 46.

20. Knight, The Ethics of Competition, p. 47.

21. Knight, The Ethics of Competition, p. 62.

22. See Israel M. Kirzner, Competition and Entrepreneurship (Chicago: University of Chicago Press,1973), pp. 170-174.

23. See John K. Galbraith, The New Industrial State, rev. ed. (New York: Houghton Mifflin, 1971), p. 202n.

24. F. A. Hayek, "The Non-Sequitur of the Dependence Effect," Southern Economic Journal, vol. 27(1961), pp. 346-348.

25. Knight, The Ethics of Competition, p. 63.

26. See John von Neumann and Oskar Morgenstern, Theory of Games and Economic Behavior, 3rd ed.(Princeton: Princeton University Press, 1953), pp. 188-189.

27. Albert Z. Carr, "Is Business Bluffing Ethical?" Harvard Business Review, vol. 46 #1(1968), pp. 143-153. A revised version appeared in Albert Z. Carr, Business as a Game (New York: New American Library Mentor, 1969).

28. Quoted in Timothy B. Blodgett, "Showdown on Business Bluffing," Harvard Business Review, vol. 46 #3(1968). Reprinted as Appendix to Business as a Game (see previous note), pp. 204-218. Citations from reprint, p. 217.

29. Carr, quoted in Blodgett, "Showdown...," p. 217.

30. Carr, Business as a Game, p. 145. See John McDonald, Strategy in Poker, Business and War (New York: W. W. Norton, 1950), p. 44.

31. John McDonald has some good thoughts on this in The Game of Business (Garden City: Doubleday, 1975), pp. 104-127.

32. F. A. Hayek, Law, Legislation and Liberty, vol. 2 (Chicago: University of Chicago Press, 1976), p. 73. In his footnote, Hayek cites the works of three early Jesuits, Luis Molina, Johannes de Salas, and Juan de Lugo. History has its ironies.

33. See Robert Lipsyte, "Pleasures of the Flesh," Newsweek, June 23, 1975, p. 13.

34. F. A. Hayek, "The Meaning of Competition," in Individualism and the Economic Order (London: Routledge and Kegan Paul, 1949); and P. J. McNulty, "A Note on the History of Perfect Competition," Journal of Political Economy, vol. 75(1967, p. 398, and "The Meaning of Competition," Quarterly Journal of Economics, vol. 82 (1968), pp. 638-656.

35. Joseph A. Schumpeter, Capitalism, Socialism and Democracy (New York: Harper and Row, 1962), p. 84.

36. See table, Michael Maccoby, The Gamesman (New York: Simon and Schuster, 1976), p. 104.

37. Knight, The Ethics of Competition, p. 47.

38. Knight, The Ethics of Competition, p. 68.

39. See the slightly different comments on this by Eugene V. Rostow, "The Ethics of Competition Revisited," p. 331.

NOTES FOR CHAPTER SIX

1. I have here used A. A. Berle extensively: Power without Property (New York: Harcourt, Brace and World, 1959), pp. 82-83; and The 20th Century Capitalist Revolution (New York: Harcourt, Brace and World Harvest Book, 1954), pp. 32-35.

2. A. A. Berle, The 20th Century Capitalist..., p. 65.

3. See Abraham Kaplan, American Ethics and Public Policy (New York: Oxford, 1963), p. 77.

4. "Power,""potency,""potentiality,""ability" and such terms are all interrelated and interdefined, so that, unless one can point to some immediate experience and isolate what in the experience such words refer to, to use them does not communicate.

5. John Locke, Essay on Human Understanding, II, 7, #8.

6. Sigmund Freud, Civilization and Its Discontents (New York: W. W. Norton, 1961), pp. 13-14.

7. Thomas Hobbes, Leviathan, I, chapter 11.

8. William Wordsworth, "Rob Roy's Grave."

9. Thucydides, The Peloponnesian War, V, 105, 2. I recommend the excellent study by A. Geoffrey Woodhead, Thucydides on the Nature of Power (Cambridge: Harvard University Press, 1970).

10. Bertrand Russell, Power (London: George Allen and Unwin, 1938), p. 25.

11. Herbert Goldhamer and Edward A. Shils, "Types of Power and Status," The American Journal of Sociology, vol. 45 #2(1939), pp. 171-182. See also Peter Lasswell and Abraham Kaplan, Power and Society (New Haven: Yale, 1950), p. 75.

12. Arthus S. Miller, Private Governments and the Constitution (Santa Barbara: Center for the Study of Democratic Institutions, 1959), p. 1.

13. A. A. Berle, Power without Property, p. 81.

14. Carl Kaysen, "The Corporation: How Much Power? What Scope?" in Edward S. Mason, The Corporation in Modern Society (New York: Atheneum, 1966), p. 85.

15. "Developmental" and "Extractive" are terms of C. B. Macpherson. See note 17 following.

16. David G. Winter, The Power Motive (New York: Free Press, 1973), p. 5.

17. C. B. Macpherson, Democratic Theory: Essays in Retrieval (London: Oxford, 1973), pp. 40-52.

18. Peter Drucker, The Concept of the Corporation (New York: John Day, 1946), pp. 6-7, n.1.

19. Abram Chayes, "The Modern Corporation and the Rule of Law," in Edward S. Mason, The Corporation in...," pp. 25,26,27.

20. See Martin Heidegger on "heritage," Sein und Zeit, trans. Being and Time (New York: Harper and Row, 1962), Sein und Zeit, p. 383; Being and Time, p. 435.

21. A. A. Berle, The American Economic Republic (New York: Harcourt, Brace and World Harvest book, 1963), p. 42.

22. A. A. Berle, The American Economic Republic, pp. 42-43.

23. Abram Chayes, "The Modern Corporation...," p. 31.

24. Peter Drucker, The Age of Discontinuity (New York: Harper and Row, 1968), pp. 24-28; 40; 96; 171.

25. C. B. Macpherson, Democratic Theory, pp. 3-23.

26. John Rawls, A Theory of Justice (Cambridge: The Belknap Press, 1971), pp. 426-427.

27. A. A. Berle, The 20th Century Capitalist..., pp. 29-32.

28. "Who Owns American Industry? The Big Shifts Underway,"
U.S. News and World Report, July 18, 1977, pp. 70-71; "Are the
Institutions Wrecking Wall Street?" Business Week, June 2, 1973,
p. 58. See also, A. A. Berle, "The New Realities of Corporate
Power," Dun's Review, vol. 92 #6 (Dec., 1968), pp. 43-45, 80,
reprinted in Fred Luthans and Richard M. Hodgetts, Social Issues
in Business (New York: Macmillan, 1972), pp. 46-51.
   29. A. A. Berle, The American Economic Republic, pp. 26-29.
   30. A. A. Berle, The American Economic Republic, p. 25.
   31. A. A. Berle, The American Economic Republic, p. 32.
   32. A. A. Berle, Power (New York: Harcourt, Brace and World,
1967), pp. 39-132.

NOTES FOR CHAPTER SEVEN

   1. Joseph W. McGuire, "The Social Responsibility of the Corporation," from Evolving Concepts in Management, Proceedings of
the 24th Annual Meeting, Academy of Management (Dec., 1964),
pp. 21-28. Reprinted in Fred Luthans and Richard M. Hodgetts,
Social Issues in Business (New York: Macmillan, 1972), pp. 38-
46, at pp. 40-41.
   2. A. A. Berle, "What the GNP Doesn't Tell Us," Saturday
Review (August 31, 1968), pp. 10-12.
   3. Milton Friedman, "The Social Responsibility of Business
is to Increase Its Profits," The New York Times Magazine, Sept.
13, 1970, p. 33. That he has not much changed, compare his
Capitalism and Freedom (Chicago: University of Chicago Press,
Phoenix, 1962), p. 133, and "The Responsible Corporation: Bene-
factor or Monopolist," Fortune, Nov., 1973.
   4. Henry C. Wallich and John J. McGowan, "Stockholder Interest and the Corporation's Role in Social Polity," in William
Baumol et al., A New Rationale for Corporate Social Polity (New
York: Committee for Economic Development, 1970), pp. 39-59.
   5. Milton Friedman, "Does Business Have a Social Responsibility," Bank Administration, April, 1971, p. 14.
   6. Peter Drucker, Management (New York: Harper and Row,
1973), p. 348.
   7. Peter Drucker, Management, p. 349.
   8. Harold M. Williams, "The Challenge to Business," in
George A. Steiner, ed., Selected Major Issues in Business' Role
in Modern Society (Los Angeles: Graduate School of Management,
University of California at Los Angeles, 1973), pp. 7-8.
   9. John F. A. Taylor, "Is the Corporation Above the Law?"
Harvard Business Review, vol. 43 #2(1965), p. 126.
   10. Keith Davis and Robert Blomstrom, Business and Society:
Environment and Responsibility, 3rd ed., (New York: McGraw-Hill,
1975), p. 48.
   11. George A. Steiner, "Social Policies for Business," California Management Review, vol. 14 #2 (1965), p. 126.

12. Davis and Blomstrom, Business and Society, pp. 48-49.

13. Kenneth R. Andrews, "Can the Best Corporations be made Moral?" Harvard Business Review, vol. 51 #3 (1973), p. 59.

NOTES FOR CHAPTER EIGHT

1. Peter Drucker, Management (New York: Harper and Row, 1973), p. 368.

2. Peter Drucker, Management, p. 391-400, at 393.

3. Peter Drucker, Management, p. 394.

4. Peter Drucker, Management, p. 400.

5. Peter Drucker, Management, pp. 447-448.

6. Peter Drucker, Management, pp. 449-450.

7. "How Ethical are Businessmen?" Harvard Business Review, vol 39 #4 (1961), pp. 6-8 plus. Baumhart does an analysis of this survey and others in his book, Ethics In Business (New York: Holt, Rinehart and Winston, 1968).

8. Reported in Appendix B to Thomas McMahon, "Moral Problems in Middle Management," Catholic Theological Society of America Proceedings, vol. 20 (1965), pp. 46-49.

9. Archie B. Carroll, "Managerial Ethics: a Post-Watergate View," Business Horizons, April, 1975, pp. 75-80. A survey of Pitney-Bowes, Inc., supports Carroll's study, Business Week, January 31, 1977, p. 177.

10. Cited in "Stiffer Rules for Business Ethics," a Business Week supplement, Business Week, March 30, 1974, pp. 87-89.

11. Robert Seidenberg, Corporate Wives---Corporate Casualties? (Garden City: Doubleday Anchor, 1975), pp. xii-xiii.

12. Harrison Johnson, "How to Get the Boss's Job," Modern Office Procedure, vol. 6 #5 (1961), pp. 15-18.

13. Douglas McGregor, The Human Side of Enterprise (New York: McGraw-Hill, 1960), esp. pp. 34-48.

14. Clarence C. Walton, "Overview," The Ethics of Corporate Conduct (Englewood Cliffs, N.J.: Prentice-Hall, 1977), p. 14.

15. John J. Morse and Jay W. Lorsch, "Beyond Theory Y," reprinted in the volume Harvard Business Review: On Management (New York: Harper and Row, 1975), at p. 379.

16. See Richard J. Barnet and Ronald E. Muller, Global Reach (New York: Simon and Schuster, 1974), pp. 40-43.

17. William H. Whyte, Jr., The Organization Man (New York: Simon and Schuster, 1956), p. 3.

18. See Alvar O. Elbing and Carol Elbing, The Value Issue of Business (New York: McGraw-Hill, 1967), pp. 86-90.

19. Henry Davis, S.J., Moral and Pastoral Theology (London: Sheed and Ward, 1949), I, p. 93.

20. On the developments in the legal nuances of "agency," see Phillip I. Blumberg, "Corporate Responsibility and the Employee's Duty of Loyalty and Obedience: A Preliminary Inquiry," Oklahoma Law Review, August, 1971, reprinted in Dow Votaw and S. Prakash Sethi, The Corporate Dilemma (Englewood Cliffs, N.J.:

Prentice-Hall, 1973), pp. 82-113. Citations from book.

21. James M. Roche, "The Competitive System, To Work, To Pre-
serve, and To Protect," Vital Speeches of the Day, May 1, 1971,
p. 445.

22. Phillip I. Blumberg, "Corporate Responsibility...," pp.
82-83.

23. See Charles Peters and Taylor Branch, Blowing the Whistle:
Dissent in the Public Interest (New York: Praeger, 1972), p. 4.

24. Modified from ideas in Ralph Nader et al., Whistle Blowing (New York: Grossman, 1972), p. 5.

25. Kenneth D. Walters, "Your employees' right to blow the
whistle," Harvard Business Review, vol. 53 #4 (1975), pp. 26-
34, 161-162, at p. 27.

26. Thomas I. Emerson, The System of Freedom of Expression
(New York: Vintage, 1970), p. 677.

27. Phillip I. Blumberg, "Corporate Responsibility...," p. 82.

28. Modified from ideas in Ralph Nader, et al., Whistle Blow-
ing, p. 6, and Keith Davis and Robert Blomstrom, Business and
Society: Environment and Responsibility, 3rd ed. (New York:
McGraw-Hill, 1975), pp. 175-176.

NOTES FOR CHAPTER NINE

1. James Webb Young, "Wanted: Responsible Advertising Crit-
ics," Saturday Review, April 23, 1960, pp. 35ff.

2. Donald L. Kanter, "Psychological Considerations in Advertising Regulation," in S. Prakash Sethi, ed., The Unstable
Ground: Corporate Social Policy in a Dynamic Society (Los Angeles: Melville, 1974), pp. 448-457.

3. Donald L. Kanter, "Psychological ...," p. 454.

4. John K. Galbraith, The Affluent Society (New York: New
American Library Mentor, 1958), p. 117.

5. John K. Galbraith, The Affluent Society, p. 124.

6. John K. Galbraith, The Affluent Society, p. 127.

7. John K. Galbraith, The Affluent Society, p. 128.

8. John K. Galbraith, "Economics and the Quality of Life,"
Science, vol. 145 (July 10, 1961), pp. 346-348.

9. F. A. Hayek, "The Non-Sequitur of the 'Dependence Effect,'" Southern Economic Journal, vol. 27 (1961), pp. 346-348.

10. Ronald Gross, "The Language of Advertising."

11. Theodore Levitt, "The Morality (?) of Advertising," Harvard Business Review, vol. 48 #4 (1970), pp. 84-92, at p. 85.

12. Theodore Levitt, "The Morality...," p. 89.

13. Theodore Levitt, "The Morality...," p. 91.

14. George Orwell, "Politics and the English Language."